JAPANESE
for Business

JAPANESE
for Business

Chris Dillon

Hugo's Language Books Limited

'Japanese for Business' is also available in a pack
with four cassettes: ISBN 0 85285 241 X

Written by

Chris Dillon B.A. Hons. Japanese

Information Librarian
Daiwa Anglo-Japanese Foundation, London

Cover photo: The Ginza, Tokyo (Robert Harding Picture Library)

Set in Helvetica 55 & 65 by
Typesetters Limited, Hertford
Printed and bound in Great Britain by
Page Brothers, Norwich, Norfolk

PREFACE

The aim of this book is to equip the business traveller with a basic grasp of the Japanese language. Particular emphasis is placed upon dialogues and vocabulary appropriate to the kinds of situations that business people visiting Japan will meet. Guidance is given on various sources of business information and points of business etiquette, together with more general advice on planning a trip to Japan.

The course is designed to meet the needs of the business person with relatively little time to spare for language study. For this reason, no attempt has been made to cover the Japanese script, which requires many hundreds of hours to learn. Incidentally, it is largely the complexity of the script, rather than any inherent difficulty in the grammar or pronunciation, which gives Japanese its reputation as a 'difficult' language. For those with the time and inclination to delve deeper into the language, suggestions for further study are given in the Information section of Unit Seven.

The course introduces all the patterns or 'structures' most frequently used in Japanese. Each Unit introduces a part of speech or basic form and illustrates the various structures in which it occurs. Vocabulary has been broken down into constituent parts and related to other useful vocabulary where this is likely to be helpful to the learner.

When using the course, the learner is advised to study the vocabulary attached to each Structure or Conversation first, so that as much attention as possible may be directed towards the actual usage in the boxed model sentences, the Fluency Practices and the Conversations.

I would like to take this opportunity to offer my profound thanks to all those who helped to bring this book to completion: to Yasuko Okamoto, Takeshi Shimizu, and John and Chika Breen for their invaluable assistance; to Ruth Nason for her patient and painstaking editing; and to my wife Rachel for her suggestions and support. Responsibility for any errors in the book is of course mine alone.

CONTENTS

THE PRONUNCIATION OF JAPANESE

The basic unit of pronunciation in Japanese is the syllable, rather than the consonant or the vowel. Vowels occur as syllables on their own or preceded by a consonant (sometimes plus 'y'). Consonants do not occur without a vowel following (except in the case of 'n').

Vowels

The Japanese vowels are **a**, **i**, **u**, **e** and **o**. They occur both long and short. Long vowels last twice as long as short vowels. When Japanese is written in the Roman alphabet, long 'a', 'u' and 'o' are usually written with a 'macron' (bar) over them: **ā**, **ū**, **ō**. However, long 'i' and 'e' are spelled **ī** and **ē** only in foreign words such as **chīzu** ('cheese') and **kēsu** ('case'). Usually they are spelled **ii** and **ei**, as in **ii** ('good') and **Eigo** ('English').

Pronouncing a vowel long when it should be short or vice versa is likely to cause considerable confusion.

a	as in 'cat': **karate, karaoke**
ā	as in 'father': **Shāpu** ('Sharp')
i	as in 'eat' but shorter. The vowel in 'it' is rather different from the Japanese sound, but would be understood: **origami**
ii or **ī**	as in 'eat': **chīzu** ('cheese'), **sararīman** ('businessman'; lit., 'salary man')
u	as in 'put': **Suzuki, samurai**
ū	as in 'boot', but spread your lips as you say it! **jūdō, jūjutsu**
e	as in 'get': **terebi** ('television')
ei or **ē**	as in 'eight' – except that the Japanese vowel is a pure sound; the English is a diphthong ending in an 'i' sound: **Seikō, dētabēsu** ('database')

o   as in 'off', NOT as in 'owe':
Toyota

ō   as in 'bought':
sumō, Tōkyō

ai   as in 'pie', NOT as in 'pay':
aisɯkurīmu ('ice-cream'), **bonsai**

'   Occasionally, two short vowels are pronounced one after the other without forming a diphthong or long vowel. When this happens, an apostrophe has been inserted: **cha'iro** ('brown'), **i'in-kai** ('committee')

Devoiced vowels

Some Japanese 'u's and 'i's are devoiced (pronounced faintly). Vowels which are so faint that they are, to all intents and purposes, silent have been marked 'ɯ' and 'ɨ' in this book. Unfortunately, many dictionaries and text books do not state whether 'u' and 'i' are silent. These are the rules of thumb:

1   Devoicing does not usually happen when the vowel starts or ends a word.
    The major exceptions to this rule are the verb **desɯ** ('is') and the common verb ending **-masɯ**.
    Note that **desɯ** and **-masɯ** are occasionally pronounced **desu** and **-masu**; for example, before **ne** and **ga**.
2   In foreign words, 'u's and 'i's not present in the original are usually devoiced. For example: **Fɯransu** ('France'). There is no 'u' sound after the 'F' in 'France', so the inserted Japanese 'u' is devoiced. Note, however, that the inserted 'u' at the end of the word is not devoiced (Rule 1).

Consonants: 1

The following consonants are similar to those found in English: **b, d, g** (at the beginning of a word), **m, n** (at the beginning of a syllable), **s, z, sh, j, y**.

The following consonants are similar to in English but are pronounced with less aspiration. (If you listen carefully, there is a small puff of breath, or 'aspiration', after these consonants in English when they are pronounced before a vowel): **p**, **t**, **k**, **ch**.

Consonant and vowel combinations

ba	**bi**	**bu**	**be**	**bo**	
da	***di**	***du**	**de**	**do**	
ga	**gi**	**gu**	**ge**	**go**	
ma	**mi**	**mu**	**me**	**mo**	
na	**ni**	**nu**	**ne**	**no**	
sa		**su**	**se**	**so**	'si' is rendered as **shi**.
za		**zu**	**ze**	**zo**	'zi' is rendered as **ji**.
sha	**shi**	**shu**	***she**	**sho**	
ja	**ji**	**ju**	***je**	**jo**	
ya		**yu**	***ye**	**yo**	'yi' is rendered as **i**.
ha			**he**	**ho**	See 'Consonants: 2' for **hi**;
pa	**pi**	**pu**	**pe**	**po**	'hu' is rendered as **fu**.
ta	***ti**		**te**	**to**	'tu' is rendered as **tsu**.
ka	**ki**	**ku**	**ke**	**ko**	
cha	**chi**	**chu**	***che**	**cho**	

*These syllables occur only in foreign words.

Consonants: 2
The following consonants are dissimilar to those found in English: **h** (before 'i' or 'y'), **f**, **r**, **g** (between vowels), **ts**, **w**, **n** (as a syllable on its own), **consonant y vowel**.

h (before 'i' or 'y' – see also **Consonant 'y' vowel**): Whereas the 'h' in **ha**, **he** and **ho** is pronounced similarly to 'h' in English, in **hi** and **hy** it is formed further back in the mouth. It is similar to the consonant in German 'ich'. English 'h' is always understandable, however.
Hiroshima, Hitachi, Hirohito, hyō ('[mathematical, etc.] table')

fa, fi, fu, fe, fo: Japanese 'f' is made by using both lips, not by using the top teeth and lower lip as in English. Imagine you are blowing out a candle! English 'f' is always understandable.
Fuji, fōku ('fork'), **firumu** ('film'), **futon**

ra, ri, ru, re, ro: 'R' is probably the most difficult Japanese sound for English speakers to produce. It is made by the tongue striking the gum behind the top front teeth. But don't leave it there too long or you will produce a 'd'! English 'r' is usually understandable.
rajio ('radio'), **rizumu** ('rhythm'), **rejā** ('leisure')

g (between vowels): When 'g' occurs between two vowels, it is pronounced as 'ng' in 'ring'. If you find this difficult, just use English 'g', as many young Japanese people do.
Nagasaki

tsu: This is a 't' sound followed immediately by an 's' sound and the vowel 'u'. It is similar to the 'z' sound in German 'Zeitgeist'. It is NOT the same sound as 'su'.
Mitsubishi, Mitsui

wa, wi, we, wo: Japanese 'w' is not pronounced as strenuously as its English counterpart. However, the latter would always be understandable.
Shōwa, wisukī ('whisky')

n (when it forms a syllable on its own): This is pronounced 'ng' (as in English 'ring') except before 'd', 't', 'n' and 'r', when it is pronounced 'n'; and before 'b', 'm' and 'p', when it is pronounced 'm'.
Honda (-n-), **Nissan** (-ng), **shinbun** (-m-) ('newspaper')

When this 'n' is followed immediately by a vowel, an apostrophe is inserted to avoid confusion with **na, ni, nu, ne** and **no**.
sen'en ('¥1,000'), **ichi-man'en** ('¥10,000')

In fact, the above often sound like **sengyeng** and **ichimangyeng**, with a slight 'y' inserted to make them easier to say.

Consonant 'y' vowel: Apart from occurring in **ya, yu, ye** and **yo**, as mentioned above, Japanese 'y' also occurs after some consonants and before 'a', 'u' and 'o', as follows:

bya	byu	byo		pya	pyu	pyo
gya	gyu	gyo		kya	kyu	kyo
mya	myu	myo		hya	hyu	hyo
nya	nyu	nyo		rya	ryu	ryo

Tōkyō, Kyōto

Double consonants

ss, ssh (double 'sh'), **pp, tt, tch** (double 'ch'), **kk, bb*, dd*, gg***
*These double consonants occur only in foreign words.

Double consonants occur only in the middle of words. In actual pronunciation, the first consonant is not fully pronounced; the mouth goes into the position required, stays there momentarily and then produces the second consonant.

As with vowel length, pronouncing a double consonant as a single one will cause considerable confusion; so please pay particular attention to both of these points right from the beginning!
Nissan, Irasshaimase (greeting used by shop assistants et al.), **ossharu** ('say', 'be called'); **happyō** ('announcement'), **yappari** ('as expected'); **Chotto matte kudasai** ('Please wait a moment'), **itta** ('went' or 'said'); **suitchi** ('switch'); **Kekkō desψ** ('No thank you'), **kekkon** ('marriage'); **beddo** ('bed'); **baggu** ('bag')

No 'l', 'v' or 'th'
Note that 'l', 'v' and 'th' do not exist in Japanese. Foreign words containing these consonants replace 'l', 'v' and 'th' with Japanese 'r', 'b' and 'z' (sometimes 's').
raion ('lion'), **bideo** ('video'), **Satchā** ('Thatcher'), **za** ('the')

Stress and pitch
Most English words of more than one syllable have some syllables stressed more heavily than others: for example, 'father', where the 'a' is stressed and the 'er' unstressed. In Japanese, it is important to stress all syllables (except those containing devoiced vowels) evenly.

If you have a good ear, you may notice that, although Japanese intonation is generally rather flat, some syllables in Japanese are pitched slightly higher than others; for example, the 'na' in **nan** of **Nan desψ ka** ('What is it?'). The rules for this are complex and learners need not concern themselves with them at this stage. Japanese is not a tone language, unlike Chinese, and incorrect use of pitch is not a barrier to comprehension.

Hyphens

Hyphens have been used in this book to split long words into recognizable smaller parts: for example, **Nihon-jin** ('a Japanese person') – showing that the word is formed from **Nihon** ('Japan') and **-jin**, a suffix meaning 'person'.

Spelling English words

If you need to spell English words, for example your name, in Japanese, it is safest to use the following pronunciations for the letters of the Roman alphabet:

A	**ē**	N	**enu**
B	**bī**	O	**ō**
C	**shī**	P	**pī**
D	**dī**	Q	**kyū**
E	**ī**	R	**āru**
F	**efu**	S	**esu**
G	**jī**	T	**tī**
H	**eichi**	U	**yū**
I	**ai**	V	**bui**
J	**jē**	W	**daburyu**
K	**kē**	X	**ekkɰsu**
L	**eru**	Y	**wai**
M	**emu**	Z	**zetto**

UNIT ONE

In this first Unit we will meet the Japanese verb for 'to be' and learn the basic usage of **wa**, **mo** and **no**. We will practise asking basic questions and reading numbers out aloud. And we will see how to turn the form of verbs given in Japanese dictionaries into the form used by Japanese people in everyday language.

Structure 1: desʉ

Deibiddo Sʉmisu desʉ.
I <u>am</u> David Smith.
Bʉraun-san desʉ.
She <u>is</u> Mrs Brown.
Igirisu-jin desʉ.
We <u>are</u> British.
Nihon-jin desʉ.
They <u>are</u> Japanese.
Jānarisʉto desʉ.
We <u>are</u> journalists.
Bengo-shi desʉ.
I <u>am</u> a lawyer.

CHECKNOTES 1

a) **Desʉ** means '(I) am', '(you) are', '(he, she, it) is', '(we) are', '(you) are', '(they) are', depending on the context.

b) In Japanese, the verb always comes at the end of the sentence. It is not necessary to specify the subject or topic if it is clear from the context.

c) **-san** attached to other people's names is roughly equivalent to 'Mr', 'Mrs', 'Miss'.

d) **-jin** attached to the name of a country gives the word for the inhabitant of that country. For example, **Amerika** is 'America' and **Amerika-jin** is 'American (person)'.

e) Note that there is no precise Japanese equivalent to English 'a' and 'the'. Moreover, most Japanese words have no plural. For example, **bengo-shi** could mean 'a/the lawyer' or '(the) lawyers' in context.

Checklist 1

Amerika-jin	American (person)
Doitsu-jin	German (person)
Fшransu-jin	French (person)
Igirisu-jin	British (person)
Nihon-jin	Japanese (person)
bengo-shi	lawyer
dezainā	designer
jānarisшto	journalist
kaikei-shi	accountant
kōmu-in	civil servant
sensei	teacher

FLUENCY PRACTICE 1

Translate the following sentences into English:

1 Jon Howaito (John White) desш.
2 Amerika-jin desш.
3 Dezainā desш.
4 Rinda Teirā (Linda Taylor) desш.
5 Doitsu-jin desш.

Translate the following sentences into Japanese:

6   I am a teacher.
7   He is Mr Watt (**Watto-san**).
8   They are accountants.
9   You are French.
10 We are civil servants.

Check your answers with the key on page 187.

Structure 2: wa (the topic)

Kore <u>wa</u> pasψpōto desψ.
This is a passport.
Sore <u>wa</u> konpyūtā desψ.
That is a computer.
Are <u>wa</u> denwa desψ.
That (over there) is a telephone.
Watashi <u>wa</u> Itaria-jin desψ.
I am Italian.
Kawaguchi-san <u>wa</u> enjinia desψ.
Mr/Mrs/Miss Kawaguchi is (or 'you are' in context) an engineer.
Kare <u>wa</u> Doitsu-jin desψ.
He is German.
Kanojo <u>wa</u> hisho desψ.
She is a secretary.
Watashi-tachi <u>wa</u> Nihon-jin desψ.
We are Japanese.
Kare-ra <u>wa</u> bengo-shi desψ.
They are lawyers.
Kanojo-tachi <u>wa</u> Igirisu-jin desψ.
They (female) are British.

CHECKNOTES 2

a) **Wa** indicates the topic of the sentence. This is not always the same as the subject! Topics are only expressed in Japanese when they are not obvious. So, for example, if there are two sentences with the same topic, the second sentence does not repeat it. For example, 'I am Jane. I am British' is: **Watashi wa Jēn desψ. Igirisu-jin desψ.** (NOT **Watashi wa Jēn desψ. Watashi wa Igirisu-jin desψ.**)

b) Japanese for 'you' is **anata**. However, this is used much less frequently than its English equivalent. If you know the surname of the person you are addressing, it is politer to use this (plus -**san**) than **anata**. An English parallel might be 'One lump of sugar or two, *Mrs Smith*?' as opposed to 'Would *you* like one lump of sugar or two?' Thus **Takahashi-san wa enjinia desψ** could mean 'You are an engineer, Mr Takahashi', when addressed to Mr Takahashi.

c) In the case of Western people, it is also possible to use the first name with -**san**. It is usually best not to use Japanese people's first names, as this sounds too familiar.

Checklist 2

are	that (one) (over there)
kore	this (one)
sore	that (one) (already mentioned)
watashi	I
kare	he
kanojo	she
watashi-tachi	we
kare-ra	they
kanojo-tachi	they (referring to a group of women)
Chūgoku-jin	Chinese (person)
Itaria-jin	Italian (person)
chiketto	ticket (for cinema, theatre, etc.)
denwa	telephone
enjinia	engineer
hikō-ki	plane (from **hikō**, 'flight', and **-ki**, 'machine')
hisho	secretary
kamera	camera
konpyūtā	computer
pasɯpōto	passport
seiji-ka	politician (**seiji** means 'politics')

FLUENCY PRACTICE 2
Translate the following sentences into English:

1 Kore wa chiketto desɯ.
2 Sore wa kamera desɯ.
3 Are wa hikō-ki desɯ.
4 Watashi wa Chūgoku-jin desɯ. Kare wa Igirisu-jin desɯ.
5 Watashi wa Māku Hauru (Mark Howell) desɯ. Bengo-shi desɯ.

Translate the following sentences into Japanese, presuming that the topics are not obvious and need to be stated:

6　He is an engineer.
7　She is a journalist.
8　They are politicians.
9　You (Mrs Tanaka) are a secretary.
10　We are British. They are Japanese.

Structure 3: mo ('also')

> **Kore wa kaban desᵫ. Sore mo kaban desᵫ.**
> This is a bag. That is also a bag.
> **Kore wa sūtsu desᵫ. Sore mo sutsᵫ desᵫ.**
> This is a suit. That is also a suit.
> **Kanojo wa kenchiku-ka desᵫ. Kare mo kenchiku-ka desᵫ.**
> She is an architect. He is also an architect.

CHECKNOTES 3
a) **Mo** means 'also' or 'too'. It is used instead of, not as well as, **wa**.

Checklist 3

bijinesuman	businessman
enpitsu	pencil
kaban	bag
kenchiku-ka	architect
konsarutanto	consultant
meishi	business card
nekutai	tie
pen	pen
shāpupen	propelling pencil (from **shāpu pen**shiru, 'sharp pencil')
sūtsu	suit

FLUENCY PRACTICE 3

Translate the following sentences into English:

1 Kore wa pen desψ. Sore mo pen desψ.
2 Kanojo wa Fψransu-jin desψ. Watashi-tachi mo Fψransu-jin desψ.
3 Kore wa enpitsu desψ. Are mo enpitsu desψ.
4 Watashi-tachi wa konsarutanto desψ. Kare-ra mo konsarutanto desψ.
5 Kore wa meishi desψ. Are mo meishi desψ.

Translate the following sentences into Japanese:

6 He is a shop assistant. They are also shop assistants.
7 She is American. We are also American.
8 This is a tie. That (over there) is also a tie.
9 I am a businessman. Mr Jones (**Jōnzu-san**) is also a businessman.
10 Those (over there) are propelling pencils. Those (over there) are also propelling pencils.

Structure 4: de wa arimasen ('am/are/is not')

Kore wa chiketto <u>de wa arimasen</u>.
This <u>is not</u> a ticket.
Soko wa o-tera <u>de wa arimasen</u>.
That (place) <u>is not</u> a temple.
Watashi wa Doitsu-jin <u>de wa arimasen</u>.
I <u>am not</u> German.
Kanojo wa sensei <u>de wa arimasen</u>.
She <u>is not</u> a teacher.
Kore wa naifu to fōku desψ. Hashi <u>de wa arimasen</u>.
These are knives and forks. They <u>are not</u> chopsticks.

CHECKNOTES 4

a) **De wa arimasen** means 'am not', 'are not', 'is not', etc. Unlikely as it may look, this is the negative of **desψ**!

Checklist 4

to	and (between two nouns)
koko	here, this place
soko	there, that place (already mentioned)
asoko	over there, that place (over there)
apāto	flat, apartment
depāto	department store
eki	station
fōku	fork
ginkō-ka	banker
hashi	chopsticks
Kanada-jin	Canadian (person)
kyōju	professor
naifu	knife
o-tera	(Buddhist) temple
sakka	writer
shinbun kisha	(newspaper) reporter
tori-shimari-yaku	director
yakɯsoku	agreement, promise; appointment

FLUENCY PRACTICE 4

Translate the following sentences into English:

1 Kanojo wa sakka de wa arimasen.
2 Sore wa yakɯsoku de wa arimasen.
3 Koko wa eki de wa arimasen.
4 Kare wa ginkō-ka de wa arimasen. Kyōju desɯ.
5 Asoko wa apāto de wa arimasen.

Translate the following sentences into Japanese:

6 He is not a director.
7 She is not Canadian.
8 We are not newspaper reporters.
9 This (place) is not a department store.
10 I am not American. I am British.

Structure 5: ka (questions)

Kare-ra wa sakka desɰ ka. Are they writers? **Igirisu-jin desɰ ka.** Are you British? **Sore wa mondai de wa arimasen ka.** Isn't that a problem?

CHECKNOTES 5

a) **Ka** is used to indicate that the preceding sentence is a question. One may think of it as a kind of pronounced question mark! Questions are typically spoken with a rising intonation.

Checklist 5

kaisha	company
mondai	problem
otearai	toilet
repōto	report
shachō	company president
wāpɰro	word processor

FLUENCY PRACTICE 5
Translate the following sentences into English:

1 Kore wa wapɰro desɰ ka.
2 Kare wa bijinesuman desɰ ka.
3 Kanojo wa Nihon-jin de wa arimasen ka.
4 Soko wa otearai desɰ ka.
5 Kare-ra wa kōmu-in de wa arimasen ka.

Translate the following sentences into Japanese:

6 Is that the report?
7 Is he an accountant?
8 Isn't she Miss Tanaka?
9 Aren't they German?
10 Isn't that the company?

Structure 6: nan, dare, doko ('what?', 'who?', 'where?')

O-namae wa <u>nan</u> desψ ka. Andō desψ.
<u>What</u> is your name? It is Andoh.
O-shigoto wa <u>nan</u> desψ ka. Enjinia desψ.
<u>What</u> is your occupation? I am an engineer.
Kore wa <u>nan</u> desψ ka. Sore wa bentō desψ.
<u>What</u> is this? That is a packed lunch.
Kanojo wa <u>dare</u> desψ ka. Kudō-san desψ.
<u>Who</u> is she? She is Miss Kudoh.
Ano kata wa <u>donata</u> desψ ka. Satō-shachō desψ.
Who is he? It's Mr Satoh, the company president.
Ima <u>doko</u> desψ ka. Shinjuku eki desψ.
<u>Where</u> are you now? I'm at Shinjuku station.

CHECKNOTES 6

a) **O-** is a prefix indicating respect. It is only used with certain nouns. For example, **namae** ('[my] name'), but **o-namae** ('[your, his, etc.] name') and **shigoto** ('[my] job'), but **o-shigoto** ('[your, his, etc.] job'). Words always used with 'o' are written without the hyphen in this book, for example: **otearai** ('toilet'; from **te**, 'hand', and **arau**, 'wash').

b) You may see Japanese ō spelled as 'oh' (as in 'Andoh'), 'o', 'oo', or even 'ou'.

c) Notice that job titles, such as **sensei** ('teacher') and **shachō** ('company president'), replace **-san** when talking about someone.

d) There is no Japanese word for 'it'. Therefore, 'it' needs to be supplied in the English translation in cases like: **Andō desψ** ('It is Andoh').

Checklist 6

nan	what?
dare	who?
doko	where?
donata	who? (more polite than **dare**)
ano kata	he/she (more polite than **kare** and **kanojo**)

22

bentō	packed lunch
chizu	map
ima	now
kaisha-in	company employee

FLUENCY PRACTICE 6

Translate the following sentences into English:

1 O-namae wa nan desψ ka. Maikeru Gψrīn (Michael Green) desψ.
2 O-shigoto wa nan desψ ka. Bijinesuman desψ.
3 Sore wa nan desψ ka. Chizu desψ.
4 Kare wa dare desψ ka. Eriotto-san (Mr Elliott) desψ.
5 Koko wa doko desψ ka. Eki desψ.

Translate the following sentences into Japanese (square brackets indicate words you don't need to translate):

6 Who is she? She's Miss Murayama.
7 Who is he? He is John (**Jon**).
8 Who (use **donata** rather than **dare**) is the company president? [It] is Mr Okutsu.
9 Where are we? (literally, 'Where is this place?') [It]'s Musashino Precision Machines (**Musashino Seimitsu Kiki**).
10 Who is she? She is Ms Baker (**Bēkā-san**).

Structure 7: no

Tōkyō wa Nihon no shuto desψ.
Tokyo is the capital of Japan.
Watashi no konpyūtā desψ.
It is my computer.
Dare no meishi desψ ka.
Whose business card is it?
Himeji Denki no shachō desψ.
He is the president of Himeji Electric.
Sore wa dare no chizu desψ ka. Toyoda-san no desψ.
Whose map is that? It's Mr/Mrs/Miss Toyoda's.

CHECKNOTES 7

a) **No** often translates as 'of' or 'from', but note the word order! **No** comes <u>after</u> the noun.

b) In a business situation, one normally introduces oneself using this word order: ORGANIZATION **no** SURNAME **desψ** ('I am SURNAME from ORGANIZATION'). For example, **Mitsubishi no Seki desψ** ('I am Seki from Mitsubishi').

c) **No** may sometimes be used in place of a noun. For example, **Sore wa dare no hon desψ ka. <u>Watashi no desψ</u>**. ('Whose book is that? <u>It's mine</u>.) This is a more natural answer than **Watashi no hon desψ** ('It's my book').

Checklist 7

Igirisu	United Kingdom (originally from 'English')
kōto	coat
Nihon	Japan
shushō	Prime Minister
shuto	capital

FLUENCY PRACTICE 7

Translate the following sentences into English:

1 Watashi no kaban desψ.
2 Kare no pasψpōto desψ.
3 Rondon ('London') wa Igirisu no shuto desψ.
4 Kore wa Tōkyō no chizu desψ ka.
5 Kare wa Nagoya Jidōsha ('Automobiles') no tori-shimari-yaku desψ.

Translate the following sentences into Japanese:

6 Who is the Prime Minister of Japan?
7 Whose business card is that? [It]'s Mr Smith's (**Sψmisu-san**) card.
8 Who does the computer belong to? That is Mr Yamaguchi's.
9 Is he the president of Akasaka Machinery (**Kikai**)?
10 Whose is that coat? That is Miss Kawajima's coat.

Structure 8: bangō (numbers)

Denwa bangō wa nan-ban desψ ka. 03-3456 7892 **(zero san [pause] san yon go roku [no] nana hachi kyū ni) desψ.**
What is your telephone number? It's 03-3456 7892.
Heya bangō wa nan-ban desψ ka. 379 **(san nana kyū) desψ.**
What is your room number? It is 379.
Fakkψsu bangō wa nan-ban desψ ka. 03-3844 7765 **(zero san [pause] san hachi yon yon [no] nana nana roku go) desψ.**
What is your fax number? It is 03-3844 7765.
Kurejitto kādo no bangō wa nan-ban desψ ka. 4977 9830 4566 3422 **(yon kyū nana nana [no] kyū hachi san zero [no] yon go roku roku [no] san yon ni ni) desψ.**
What is your credit card number? It is 4977 9830 4566 3422.

CHECKNOTES 8

a) Numbers are rather difficult in Japanese. Different sets of numbers are used in different situations, often depending on the shape of the things being counted! The list below shows the words most often used to represent the numbers 0-10 in Japanese. From now on we will treat these as the regular forms, and only note other forms as they appear.

Regular forms of numbers (0-10):

zero	zero	**roku**	six
ichi	one	**nana**	seven
ni	two	**hachi**	eight
san	three	**kyū**	nine
yon	four	**jū**	ten
go	five		

b) Some people say **rei** ('zero'), and older people may say **maru**.

c) The above regular forms are used for reading numbers such as telephone numbers aloud. When reading numbers with spaces, **no** is often used to indicate the space. For example, 0171-636 1234 would be **zero ichi nana ichi** (pause) **roku san roku (no) ichi ni san yon**.

d) When counting from one to ten, the irregular forms **shi** and **shichi** are usually used instead of **yon** ('four') and **nana** ('seven').

Checklist 8

bangō	number
fakkᵤsu	fax; fax machine
heya	room
kagi	key
kᵤrejitto kādo	credit card
nan-ban	what number?

FLUENCY PRACTICE 8

Translate the following sentences into English:

1 Nan-ban desᵤ ka. 8749 (hachi nana yon kyū) desᵤ.
2 Heya bangō wa nan-ban desᵤ ka. 574 (go nana yon) desᵤ.
3 Denwa bangō wa nan-ban desᵤ ka. Tōkyō 03-3745 9487 (zero san [pause] san nana yon go [no] kyū yon hachi nana) desᵤ.

Translate the following sentences into Japanese:

4 What is your credit card number? [It] is 4500 3498 3657 8942.
5 What is your telephone number? [It] is 0171-323 4579.
6 What is the number of the key? [It] is 54872.

Structure 9: ikura ('how much?')

Sore wa ikura desᵤ ka. ¥3,000 (sanzen'en) desᵤ.
How much is that? It is ¥3,000.
Zeikin wa ikura desᵤ ka. ¥8,147 (hassen-hyaku-yon-jū-nana-en) desᵤ.
How much is the tax? It's ¥8,147.
Ikura desᵤ ka. Zenbu de ¥4,340 (yon-sen-sanbyaku-yon-jū-en) desᵤ.
How much are they? They are ¥4,340 in all.
Ryōkin wa ikura desᵤ ka. ¥8,000 (hassen'en) hodo desᵤ.
How much is the charge? It's about ¥8,000.

CHECKNOTES 9

Regular forms of numbers (11-100,000,000):

jū-ichi	11
jū-ni	12
jū-san	13
ni-jū	20
ni-jū-ichi	21
ni-jū-ni	22
san-jū	30
hyaku	100
hyaku-ichi	101
hyaku-ni	102
hyaku-jū-ichi	111
hyaku-jū-ni	112
hyaku-ni-jū	120
ni-hyaku	200
sanbyaku	300
roppyaku	600
happyaku	800
sen	1,000
sanzen	3,000
hassen	8,000
ichi-man	10,000
ichi-man-sen	11,000
ichi-man-ni-sen	12,000
ni-man	20,000
jū-man	100,000
hyaku-man	1,000,000
sen-man	10,000,000
ichi-oku	100,000,000

a) Eleven is literally 'ten-one' and twenty is 'two-ten', etc., using the numbers in the 'Regular forms of numbers' list in Structure 8.

b) Note that the Japanese say **hyaku** and **sen** for 'one or a hundred' and 'one or a thousand'.

c) Japanese has a word for ten thousand: **ichi-man**. One hundred thousand, one million and ten million are **jū-man**, **hyaku-man** and **sen-man** respectively. Again Japanese has a word for one hundred million: **ichi-oku**. The forms 'jū-sen', 'hyaku-sen' and 'sen-sen' do not exist. It takes some amount of time for the concept of **-man** and **-oku** to become natural. Until it does, be very careful with large numbers in Japanese!

d) Note that sound changes occur when certain elements come together, for example: **roku** ('6') + **hyaku** ('100') becomes **roppyaku** ('600'). Cases where such sound changes occur have been underlined in the list opposite.

e) To talk about numbers of **Yen**, add **-en** to the relevant number. Note the following sound change: ¥4 = **yoen** (NOT 'yon-en').

f) **Sen'en** ('¥1,000') and **ichi-man'en** ('¥10,000') are pronounced **sengyeng** and **ichimangyeng**. (See 'Consonants: 2', page 10.)

Checklist 9

kono	this, these (followed by a noun)
sono	that, those (already mentioned) (followed by a noun)
ano	that, those (over there) (followed by a noun)

(NB: **Kore**, **sore** and **are** are never followed by nouns.)

hodo	about (follows the noun)
ikura	how much?
zenbu de	in all

kagu	furniture
kikai	machine
o-kanjō	bill
pᵤrintā	printer
ryōkin	charge
setto	set
shōhin	goods, product
tokei	clock/watch
zeikin	tax

FLUENCY PRACTICE 9

Translate the following sentences into English:

1 Meishi wa ikura desѱ ka. Go-sen-yon-hyaku-en desѱ.
2 Sono tokei wa ikura desѱ ka. Sanzen-sanbyaku-en desѱ.
3 Sono shōhin wa ikura desѱ ka. Kyū-sen-go-hyaku-en desѱ.
4 Ano pѱrintā wa ikura desѱ ka. San-man-go-sen'en desu.
5 Kono konpyūtā wa ikura desѱ ka. Hachi-man'en desѱ.

Translate the following sentences into Japanese, writing the numbers out in full:

6 How much is the bill? [It] is ¥9,450 in all.
7 How much is the charge? [It] is ¥7,490.
8 How much is the set? [It] is ¥20,500.
9 How much is the machine? [It] is ¥1,000,000.
10 How much is this furniture? [It] is about ¥1,500,000 in all.

Structure 10: Verbs

CHECKNOTES 10

a) Japanese verbs belong to two basic styles, which are referred to in this book as the Plain style and the Polite style. The Plain style is used in informal situations (for example, among close friends or members of a family). It is also used in certain grammatical structures (to be discussed as they appear in this book). The Plain present, the form in which verbs are listed in dictionaries, ends in -u. The only exception is da ('am', 'are', 'is', etc.).

The Plain style is inappropriate in most formal situations. Instead, the endings -masѱ, etc. (see Unit Two) are attached to verbs, to make the Polite style. Again, da is the only exception: its Polite present is desѱ.

b) There are two basic ways to derive the Polite present from the Plain present, depending on the ending of the Plain present.

When the Plain present ends in a consonant plus -u, the Polite present is formed as follows:

CONSONANT VERBS

Plain present		Polite present	
yo<u>B</u>.u	→	yo<u>B</u>.i.masɯ	('call')
iso<u>G</u>.u	→	iso<u>G</u>.i.masɯ	('rush')
ka<u>K</u>.u	→	ka<u>K</u>.i.masɯ	('write')
yo<u>M</u>.u	→	yo<u>M</u>.i.masɯ	('read')
↝shi<u>N</u>.u	→	shi<u>N</u>.i.masɯ	('die')
no<u>R</u>.u	→	no<u>R</u>.i.masɯ	('get on')
hana<u>S</u>.u	→	hana<u>SH</u>.i.masɯ*	('speak')
ma<u>TS</u>.u *	→	ma<u>CH</u>.i.masɯ*	('wait')
ka(<u>W</u>).u **	→	ka.<u>i</u>.masɯ	('buy')

This sort of verb is called a 'Consonant verb', as the last letter of the verb stem is a consonant.

*The syllables 'si', 'tu' and 'ti' do not exist in native Japanese words (see 'Consonants: 1', page 9), so **shi**, **tsu** and **chi** are used instead. Note that **sh**, **ts** and **ch** are treated as one consonant.

This **w is only pronounced before **a**: for example, **kawanai** ('does not buy'), a Plain present negative (see Structure 47).

When the Plain present ends in **-eru** or **-iru**†, the Polite present is formed as follows:

VOWEL VERBS

Plain present		Polite present	
tab<u>E</u>.ru	→	tab<u>E</u>.masɯ	('eat')
m<u>I</u>.ru	→	m<u>I</u>.masɯ	('see')

This sort of verb is called a 'Vowel verb', as the last letter of the verb stem is a vowel.

†There is a small number of Consonant verbs ending in **-eru** and **-iru**. These will be indicated in the Checklists as they occur. They conjugate like **no<u>R</u>.u**.

c) **Irregular Verbs**

Plain present		Polite present
da	→	**desɯ**
suru	→	**sh<u>I</u>.masɯ**
kuru	→	**k<u>I</u>.masɯ**

NOTE: From now on, all verbs will be listed in the Plain present in the Checklists.

CONVERSATION 1: Meishi kōkan
('Exchanging business cards')

Deibiddo Sɯmisu: Hajimemashᵻte. Roiyaru Fānichā no Deibiddo Sɯmisu desɯ. Yoroshᵻku o-negai shimasɯ.

Suzuki: Hajimemashᵻte. Suzuki desɯ. Yoroshᵻku o-negai shimasɯ. Dōzo o-kake kudasai.

David Smith: How do you do? I'm David Smith from Royal Furniture. Pleased to meet you.

Suzuki: How do you do? I'm Suzuki. Pleased to meet you. Please sit down.

Notes on Conversation 1

a) **Hajimemashᵻte** ('How do you do?') is a notorious tongue-twister. It may help to think of it as **hajime + mashᵻte**.

b) **Yoroshᵻku o-negai shimasɯ** in this conversation means 'Pleased to meet you'. Literally, it means 'I make a humble request' (=**o-negai shimasɯ**) 'to be treated well' (=**yoroshᵻku**).

c) **Dōzo o-kake kudasai** ('Please sit down') consists of **Dōzo** ('please') + **o-kake kudasai** ('sit down').

d) New words:
   kōkan   exchange
   Roiyaru Fānichā Royal Furniture

INFORMATION: Preparing for your trip

When to travel

The Japanese climate varies widely from season to season. Spring and autumn tend to be pleasantly warm; winter is generally crisp and bright; the summer heat, however, can be quite oppressive, due to the high degree of humidity. For this reason, business trips in July and August are best avoided if at all possible. If you do have to visit Japan during the summer months, you should bear in mind that clothes will have to be pressed frequently, since they will crumple easily in the humidity.

National holidays should be taken into account when planning a trip. Virtually all commercial activity ceases during the New Year period and the first week of May (Golden Week). There are also occasional one-day national holidays throughout the year, and it would be advisable to check the dates of these before booking your trip.

Visas

Tourist visas (valid for 90 days) will normally be granted automatically on entry into Japan. However, if you intend to engage in any commercial activity during your trip, you will need to apply in advance for a business visa (valid for up to three years).

If in any doubt as to whether you need a visa, consult the Consular Section at the Japanese Embassy. Note that if you enter Japan with the wrong type of visa, you may have to leave the country in order to change it.

Costs

Tokyo is perhaps the most expensive business capital in the world. Many an unwary traveller has been caught out by unexpectedly large bills. Particular care should be taken when entertaining out, even if this is to be charged to a company expense account!

The most convenient method of payment is by credit card. Travellers' cheques are a mixed blessing: not every Japanese bank will handle them, and those that do can be remarkably slow. However, most major hotels will change them.

Health insurance

When arranging travel insurance, bear in mind that Japan's medical charges are the highest in the world. A couple of fillings could set you back several hundred pounds! Westerner-friendly doctors, dentists and hospitals advertise in the *Japan Yellow Pages* and *City source* (see Publications section in Unit Eight, page 185).

Hotels

The Japan National Tourist Organization (see Useful addresses section in Unit Eight, page 183) has detailed lists of accommodation in all price ranges.

If you intend to stay in Tokyo, it may be convenient to choose a hotel which is served by an airport bus. Again, information about which hotels are served is available from the Japan National Tourist Organization.

Business cards

The exchange of business cards is an essential preliminary to doing business with the Japanese. It is important to have a card for everyone you meet, and if your trip involves many tours of companies, factories, or other organizations, this can mean exchanging several hundreds of cards.

It is customary to have Japanese on one side of the card. Attention should be paid to the precise translation of your job title, since this will affect how you are treated. Details of where to get Japanese cards are given in the Useful addresses section in Unit Eight, page 184.

UNIT TWO

Here we learn sentences with simple verbs in the present and past tenses; how to express the object of a verb and 'to'; how to say 'let's' and 'please give me ...'; and how to tell the time.

Structure 11: -masψ (the Polite present)

Ikimasψ ka. Hai, ikimasψ.
Are you going? Yes, I'm going.
Amerika-jin desψ ka. Iie, chigaimasψ. Igirisu-jin desψ.
Are you American? No, I'm not. I'm British.

CHECKNOTES 11

a) 'Yes' is **hai**.

b) Just as a flat 'no' in English can sound rather abrupt, so **iie** on its own can sound rude. Adding **chigaimasψ** (literally, 'it differs') is generally more polite (corresponding perhaps to 'I beg to differ').

c) Japanese has no future tense as such, so Polite present verbs ending in **-masψ** may correspond to 'I (do)', 'I'm going to (do)' or 'I shall (do)' in English. The precise meaning should be clear from the context. (This is also the case with the Plain present verbs ending in **-u** that we met in Structure 10.)

Checklist 11

au	meet
chigau	differ; no
ganbaru	do one's best
hataraku	work
iku	go
isogu	rush; be in a hurry
kaeru*	return, go back; go home
matsu	wait
wakaru	understand

*Despite the -eru ending, **kaeru** is a Consonant verb. Therefore the Polite present form is **kaerimasψ** (not 'kaemasψ', as would be expected if it were a Vowel verb).

asatte	the day after tomorrow
ashita	tomorrow
kore kara	after this
raishū	next week
kata	person (only used of other people)
yushutsu-ka	export section (from **yushutsu**, 'export', and **-ka**, 'section')

FLUENCY PRACTICE 11

Translate the following sentences into English:

1 Wakarimasψ ka. Hai, wakarimasψ.
2 Kaerimasψ ka. Hai, kore kara kaerimasψ.
3 Ganbarimasψ.
4 Asatte hatarakimasψ ka.
5 Yushutsu-ka no kata desψ ka. Iie, chigaimasψ.

Translate the following sentences into Japanese:

6 Will [you] wait? Yes, [I]'ll wait.
7 Are [you] going tomorrow?
8 [We] will meet next week.
9 Are [you] in a hurry?
10 Are [you] Mrs Katō? No, [I]'m not.

Structure 12: o (the object)

Gorufu o yarimasψ.
I play golf.
Hon/zasshi/shinbun/shōsetsu o yomimasψ.
I read a book/magazine/newspaper/novel.
Eiga/terebi o mimasψ.
I watch a film/the television.
Tegami/repōto o kakimasψ.
I write a letter/a report.
Denwa o kakemasψ.
I make a phone call.

CHECKNOTES 12

a) **O** indicates the object of the verb. It follows the noun.

b) When pronouncing a sentence like **Gorufu o yarimasѱ**, it will sound strange if you stop after **gorufu** so, as far as pronunciation is concerned, **gorufu o** may be considered one unit. **Gorufu wa, gorufu no, gorufu desѱ** and so on should also be said without pausing.

Checklist 12

kakeru	hang; **denwa o kakeru** make a phone call
kaku	write
miru	see
suu*	suck; **tabako o suu** smoke (cigarettes)
toru	take
yaru	do; play
yomu	read
eiga	film
gorufu	golf
hon	book
shashin	photo
shinbun	newspaper
shōsetsu	novel
sѱpōtsu	sport
tabako	cigarette
tegami	letter
terebi	television (originally **terebijon!**)
zasshi	magazine

* **Suu** is pronounced 'sū', with a long 'u'. The spelling **suu** makes it easier to make other verb forms.

FLUENCY PRACTICE 12

Translate the following sentences into English:

1 Sѱpōtsu o yarimasѱ.
2 Shinbun o yomimasѱ.
3 Konsarutanto wa repōto o kakimasѱ.
4 Kanojo wa denwa o kakemasѱ.
5 Tabako o suimasѱ ka.

Translate the following sentences into Japanese:
6   I write a letter.
7   We watch television.
8   I'll take a photo.
9   Will [you] write a report?
10 Will [you] make a phone call?

Structure 13: ni ('to')

Nihon <u>ni</u> ikimasɯ.
I am going <u>to</u> Japan.
Doko <u>ni</u> ikimasɯ ka.
Where are you going <u>to</u>?
Raishū Nihon <u>ni</u> shutchō shimasɯ.
I'm going on a business trip <u>to</u> Japan next week.
Murakami-san <u>ni</u> fakkɯsu o okurimasɯ.
I'll send a fax <u>to</u> Mr Murakami.

CHECKNOTES 13

a) **Ni** indicates destination ('to'). You will also hear people use **e** for the same purpose. **Ni** and **e** are usually interchangeable.

b) If **ni** or **e** (destination, indirect object) and **o** (direct object) occur in the same sentence, the noun with **ni** or **e** usually precedes the noun with **o**.

c) **Suru** ('do'/'make') is often used to turn a noun into a verb. For example, **shutchō** is 'a business trip' and **shutchō suru** is to 'go on a business trip' (literally, 'make a business trip').

Checklist 13

deru	go/come out; attend, e.g. **mītingu ni deru** attend a meeting
kuru	(irreg.: **kimasɯ**) come
okuru	send
shutchō suru	(irreg.: **shutchō shimasɯ**) go on a business trip

densha	train
hoteru	hotel
jimu-sho	office
kaigi	conference
mītingu	meeting

FLUENCY PRACTICE 13
Translate the following sentences into English:

1 Ashita Igirisu ni kaerimasɰ.
2 Tanaka-san no jimu-sho ni ikimasɰ.
3 Kono densha wa Ōtemachi ni ikimasɰ ka.
4 Nagoya ni shutchō shimasɰ.
5 Suzuki-san wa koko ni kimasɰ.

Translate the following sentences into Japanese:

6 Does this train go to Shibuya?
7 Are [you] going back to the hotel?
8 Will [you] telephone (to) me?
9 Mr Mochizuki will come after this.
10 Will [you] be attending the conference?

Structure 14: -mashita (the Polite past)

Denwa o kakemashita.
I made a telephone call.
Mītingu ni demashita ka.
Did you attend the meeting?

CHECKNOTES 14
a) The Polite past of verbs is made by changing the **-masɰ** ending to **-mashita**.

b) **Desɰ** becomes **deshita** ('was', 'were').

Checklist 14

atsumeru	collect, gather (something)
setsumei suru	explain
taberu	eat
tsukau	use
dētabēsu	database
katarogu	catalogue
ohiru	lunch
shiryō	materials, information (c.f. **jōhō**, 'intelligence', 'information')

FLUENCY PRACTICE 14
Translate the following sentences into English:

1 Kaikei-shi wa mondai o setsumei shimashita.
2 Shiryō o atsumemashita ka.
3 Ohiru o tabemashita ka.
4 Tanaka-san wa katarogu o mimashita ka.
5 Konsarutanto no repōto o yomimashita ka.

Translate the following sentences into Japanese:

6 The consultant wrote the report.
7 Did [you] buy a newspaper?
8 Have [you] sent the fax to Mr Mutō?
9 Did [you] use the database?
10 Did [my] secretary telephone?

Structure 15: -masen (the Polite present negative)

Ocha o nomi<u>masen</u>.
I don't drink Japanese tea.
Ocha o nomi<u>masen</u> ka.
Would you like some Japanese tea?
Issho ni iki<u>masen</u> ka.
Would you like to come along too?
Katō-san, ippai nomi<u>masen</u> ka.
Would you like a drink, Mr Katō?

39

CHECKNOTES 15
a) The Polite present negative of verbs is formed by changing
   -masɰ to -masen.
b) Using a sentence ending in -masen ka (literally, 'don't/won't
   you?') is often a good way to persuade somebody to do
   something.

Checklist 15

bīru	beer
ippai	one glass; ippai nomu have a drink
issho ni	together
ocha	Japanese tea
o-konomi-yaki	traditional Japanese dish, slightly resembling pizza
o-sake	rice wine; alcohol
o-sushi	sushi

FLUENCY PRACTICE 15
Translate the following sentences into English:

1 Wakarimasen.
2 Eiga o mimasen ka.
3 O-konomi-yaki o tabemasen ka.
4 O-sake o nomimasen ka.
5 Asatte Kōbe ni kaerimasen ka.

Translate the following sentences into Japanese:

6 Won't [you] wait?
7 Won't [you] eat [it]?
8 Would [you] like to play golf?
9 Would [you] like to have (use **nomu**) a beer?
10 Would [you] like to have (use **taberu**) sushi?

Structure 16: -masen deshita (the Polite past negative)

Ikimashita ka. Iie, ikimasen deshita.
Did you go? No, I didn't.
Nyūsu o kikimasen deshita.
I didn't listen to the news.

CHECKNOTES 16

a) The Polite past negative of verbs is formed by changing -masu to -masen deshita.

b) With au ('meet'), one uses ni (not o as one might expect) to indicate the person one meets: Tomodachi ni aimasen deshita ('I didn't meet my friend').

Checklist 16

kiku	hear, listen to
sansei suru	agree
buchō	department head
nyūsu	news
okusan	(your, etc.) wife
supīchi	speech; supīchi o suru make a speech
tomodachi	friend

FLUENCY PRACTICE 16

Translate the following sentences into English:

1 Gorufu o yarimashita ka. Iie, yarimasen deshita.
2 Okazaki-san wa sansei shimasen deshita.
3 Ōta-san no supīchi o kikimasen deshita.
4 Watashi-tachi wa buchō ni aimasen deshita.
5 Kurāku-san (Mr Clarke) ni fakkusu o okurimasen deshita ka.

Translate the following sentences into Japanese:

6 He didn't use the database.
7 The consultant didn't read the report.
8 Didn't [your] wife see the film?
9 Didn't the lawyer explain the problem to Mr Smith?
10 The accountants didn't attend the conference.

Structure 17: -mashō ('let's'), -mashō ka ('shall we')

Ikimashō.
Let's go.
Sō shimashō.
Let's do that.
Sore de wa, kaerimashō ka.
In that case, shall we go home?

CHECKNOTES 17
a) 'Let's' and 'shall we' are expressed by replacing **-masu** by **-mashō** and **-mashō ka** respectively.

Checklist 17

hajimeru	begin, start (something)
yameru	stop (something)
yasumu	rest
ginkō	bank
raigetsu	next month
sō	so, in that way; **sō suru** do that
sore de wa	in that case

FLUENCY PRACTICE 17
Translate the following sentences into English:

1 Hajimemashō.
2 O-sake o nomimashō ka.
3 Ganbarimashō!
4 Ginkō ni ikimashō ka.
5 Sore de wa, raigetsu aimashō.

Translate the following sentences into Japanese:

6 Let's rest.
7 Shall we go in?
8 Shall [I] read this book?
9 Shall [we] stop?
10 In that case, shall [we] play golf next month?

Structure 18: Telling the time

Ima nan-ji desɰ ka.
What time is it (now)?
Ichi-ji ni-juppun desɰ.
It is twenty past one.
Go-ji-han desɰ.
It's half past five.
Hachi-ji juppun-mae desɰ.
It's ten to eight.

CHECKNOTES 18

a) To tell the time, give the hour (**-ji**) first, followed by the minutes (**-fun**) if any, and **desɰ**.

b) Adding **nan** ('what?') gives **nan-ji** ('what time?') and **nanpun** ('how many minutes?'). Note the sound change.

c) When certain numbers (see 'Regular forms of numbers', Structures 8 and 9) are combined with **-ji** and **-fun**, the following irregular forms occur:

-ji ('o'clock'):   **yoji** ('four o'clock')
                        shichiji ('seven o'clock')
                        kuji ('nine o'clock')

-fun ('minutes'):   **ippun** ('one minute')
                        sanpun ('three minutes')
                        yonpun ('four minutes')
                        roppun ('six minutes')
                        juppun or **jippun** ('ten minutes')

d) **-han** means 'half past'. For example: **Ichi-ji-han desɰ**
('It's half past one)'.

e) **-mae** means 'to'. For example: **Shichiji juppun-mae desɰ**
('It's ten to seven').

FLUENCY PRACTICE 18
Translate the following sentences into English:

1 Ima nan-ji desɰ ka. San-ji desɰ.
2 Nan-ji desɰ ka. Jū-ichi-ji desɰ.
3 Yoji desɰ.
4 Shichiji juppun desɰ.
5 Jū-ni-ji ni-jū-go-fun desɰ.

Translate the following sentences into Japanese:

6 What time is it? It's six o'clock.
7 What time is it (now)? It's half past four.
8 It's a quarter (fifteen minutes) past eleven.
9 It's a quarter to nine.
10 It's twenty-five past seven.

Structure 19: kara ... made ('from' and 'until'/'to')

Kaigi wa jū-ji kara yoji made desɰ.
The conference is from ten o'clock until four o'clock.
Rondon kara Tōkyō made ikimasɰ.
I'll go from London to Tokyo.
Mītingu wa san-ji-han kara desɰ.
The meeting starts at (literally, 'is from') half past three.

CHECKNOTES 19
a) **Kara** ('from') and **made** ('as far as', 'until') follow the noun.

Checklist 19

kōgi   lecture
kūkō   airport

FLUENCY PRACTICE 19

Translate the following sentences into English:

1 Mītingu wa san-ji-han made desɥ.
2 Kaigi wa ashita kara hajimarimasɥ.
3 Densha wa Shinjuku eki kara demasɥ.
4 Tōkyō kara Ōsaka made ikimasɥ.
5 Kuji kara go-ji made desɥ.

Translate the following sentences into Japanese:

6 He will work until tomorrow.
7 I will go as far as Akasaka.
8 The lecture is until eight o'clock.
9 I'll go from Narita Airport to the hotel.
10 The conference is from 2.00 until 5.00.

Structure 20: kudasai ('please give me')

Sore o <u>kudasai</u>.
<u>Please give me</u> that.
Asahi Shinbun o <u>kudasai</u>.
<u>Please give me</u> an Asahi Shimbun (newspaper).
Sono zasshi o <u>o-negai shimasɥ</u>.
<u>Please give me</u> that magazine.

CHECKNOTES 20

a) ... **kudasai** is the basic way of saying 'please give me ...'.
... **o-negai shimasɥ** (literally, 'I make a humble request') is a
more polite alternative.

b) The **o**, which comes after the noun in both these expressions,
is the object **o** we met in Structure 12. It is often omitted with
o-negai shimasɥ because of the following **o**.

Checklist 20

hyaku-en-dama	a hundred Yen piece
kēki	cake
kōhī	coffee
orenji jūsu	orange juice
panfuretto	pamphlet

FLUENCY PRACTICE 20

Translate the following sentences into English:

1 Kōhī o kudasai.
2 Sono pen o kudasai.
3 Orenji jūsu o-negai shimasɰ.
4 Hyaku-en-dama o kudasai.
5 Sono kēki o kudasai.

Translate the following sentences into Japanese:

6 Please give me [some] beer.
7 Please give me that book.
8 Please give me the keys.
9 Please give me the tickets.
10 Please give me the pamphlet.

CONVERSATION 2: **Narita Kūkō nite: kippu o kau**
('At Narita Airport: buying a ticket')

Deibiddo Sᴩmisu: Shinjuku made ichi-mai o-negai shimasᴩ.
Mado-guchi no hito: Hai.
Deibiddo Sᴩmisu: Ikura desᴩ ka.
Mado-guchi no hito: ¥2,700 (Ni-sen-nana-hyaku-en) desᴩ.
Deibiddo Sᴩmisu: Dōmo.

David Smith: One ticket to Shinjuku please.
Person in booth: Yes.
David Smith: How much is it?
Person in booth: It's ¥2,700.
David Smith: Thank you.

Notes on Conversation 2

a) **Nite** ('at') follows the noun. This word is only used in titles and at the top of letters. In other cases, use **de** for 'at'.

b) **Ichi-mai** is from **ichi** ('one') + **mai** ('counter of flat things such as sheets of paper and tickets') and here means 'one ticket'. Note that object **o** is not normally used after a counter.

c) **Dōmo** ('thank you') is not very polite. It is the form often used by customers to people working in the service industries.

d) New words:
hito   person (less polite than **kata**)
mado-guchi   window (where one buys tickets, etc.)

CONVERSATION 3: **Hoteru no resepᴩshon nite: gaishutsu kara hoteru ni modoru**
('At the hotel reception: returning to the hotel after going out')

Uketsuke no hito: O-kaeri nasaimase.
Deibiddo Sᴩmisu: 1012 (Ichi zero ichi ni)-gōshitsu no Deibiddo Sᴩmisu desᴩ. Rūmu kī o o-negai shimasᴩ.
Uketsuke no hito: Hai, kochira de gozaimasᴩ.
Deibiddo Sᴩmisu: Arigatō.

Receptionist: Hello.
David Smith: I'm David Smith from room 1012. Please give
me my room key.
Receptionist: Yes, here it is.
David Smith: Thank you.

Notes on Conversation 3

a) Japanese has four **aisatsu** (salutations) used when somebody from the group leaves to go on an errand:

Itte kimasய	I'm off! (literally, 'I'm going and coming')
Itte irasshai	See you! (literally, 'Go and come')
Tadaima	I'm back! (as you return) (literally, 'just now')
O-kaeri nasai	Welcome home/back!

O-kaeri nasaimase is more polite than **o-kaeri nasai**.

b) **De gozaimasய** is the Humble form for **desய**. See Structure 30.

c) New words:

gaishutsu	going out
-gōshitsu	counter for room numbers
kochira	Polite form for **kore** ('this [one]')
modoru	return
resepயshon = uketsuke	reception
rūmu kī	(room) key

CONVERSATION 4: Resயtoran nite: Kōhī wa ikaga desய ka.
('In a restaurant: Would you like a coffee?')

Wētoresu: Kōhī wa ikaga desய ka.
Deibiddo Sயmisu: O-negai shimasய./Ie, kekkō desய.

Waitress: Would you like a coffee?
David Smith: Yes, please./No, thank you.

Notes on Conversation 4

a) **Kōhī wa ikaga desψ ka** literally means 'How is a coffee?', but **... wa ikaga desψ ka** is often used when offering things.

b) **Ie, kekkō desψ** literally means 'No. It's all right.'

c) New words:

ie	no
ikaga	how?
resψtoran	restaurant
wētoresu	waitress

CONVERSATION 5: Kissaten nite: ranchi
('At the café: lunch')

Wētoresu: Irasshaimase. Go-chūmon wa nan ni nasaimasψ ka.
Suzuki: Kyō no higawari teishoku wa nan desψ ka.
Wētoresu: A (ē) teishoku wa saba no shio-yaki de, B (bī) teishoku wa yaki-niku desψ.
Suzuki: Jā, watashi wa B teishoku o o-negai shimasψ.
Wētoresu: O-nomi-mono wa?
Suzuki: Bīru o kudasai.
Deibiddo Sψmisu: Watashi mo onaji mono o o-negai shimasψ.
Wētoresu: Hai, wakarimash+ta.

Waitress: Hello. What would you like?
Suzuki: What is today's set lunch?
Waitress: Set A is mackerel grilled in salt and Set B is grilled beef.
Suzuki: In that case, I'd like Set B, please.
Waitress: What would you like to drink?
Suzuki: Beer, please.
David Smith: The same for me, please.
Waitress: Thank you.

Notes on Conversation 5

a) **Go-chūmon wa nan ni nasaimasụ ka** means 'What would you like?' (literally, 'What will you make your order?'). **Nasaimasụ** is an example of an Honorific verb (see Structure 29).

b) **Saba no shio-yaki** is made up from **saba** ('mackerel') + **no** + **shio-yaki** ('fish grilled in salt'). **No** indicates the sort of **shio-yaki**, i.e. **saba** ('mackerel').

c) **Wakarimashıta** ('thank you') means literally 'I understood (your order)'. **Hai, wakarimashıta** is used because **hai** would feel too short.

d) New words:

... **de**	is ... and (see Structure 31)
go-chūmon	Polite word for **chūmon** order
higawari teishoku	daily menu (from **higawari**, 'daily', and **teishoku**, 'set meal'). This is usually cheaper than ordering à la carte.
irasshaimase	greeting used by shop staff et al.
jā = sore de wa	in that case
kyō	today. Note that **no** corresponds to the English 'apostrophe s' here; **kyō no higawari teishoku** today's set meal
mono	thing (physical, concrete)
O-nomi-mono wa?	What would you like to drink? (literally, '[What about] drinks?')
onaji	the same
ranchi = ohiru	lunch
yaki-niku	grilled beef (from **yaku**, 'grill', and **niku**, 'meat')

INFORMATION: Before you go

Know the organizations you will be visiting

The Japanese people you visit will expect you to be reasonably well-informed about their organizations, but will be impressed if you have obtained information which is topical.

- Companies listed on the Japanese Stock Exchanges: Information is obtainable from the quarterly *Japan Company Handbook*.

- Other companies: If the annual report is unavailable, it is possible to obtain information online from Nikkei Telecom. (Details of publications and databases are given in the Publications section in Unit Eight, page 185).

Japan Rail Pass

The Japan Rail Pass permits you to use the entire JR network at minimal cost. Buying one is a useful investment if you intend to travel widely in Japan. The pass cannot be purchased in Japan. You should obtain an exchange order, available from the Japan Centre (see the Useful addresses section in Unit Eight, page 184), which can then be converted into a pass at JR Travel Service Centres at Narita, Tokyo, Ueno, Shinjuku, Ikebukuro, Shibuya and Yokohama stations.

Japan National Tourist Organization (JNTO)

JNTO is an invaluable source of information for the traveller to Japan. It can provide free maps and information on accommodation and transport. JNTO's address is given in the Useful addresses section in Unit Eight, page 183.

Presents

When visiting organizations, it is customary to take small presents for the people who will show you round. Regional specialities or unusual items often make the best presents. British blends of tea (Earl Grey, Darjeeling, etc.), biscuits in attractive tins, or whisky, for example, are always much appreciated. And remember, you will receive numerous presents. Bear this in mind when packing before you go, in order to avoid excess luggage charges on your return!

One small point of etiquette: do not open presents in the presence of the donor. Simply look suitably overwhelmed and grateful!

No tip
Although service charges are often added to bills, as in other countries, tipping is not customary in Japan. The Japanese take great pride in providing the service at the quoted rate and may even take offence if offered a tip!

Strategies for saving money
Restaurant bills will burn a hole in your pocket alarmingly quickly. One simple way to economize is to avoid eating out in the evening. It is possible to find filling and inexpensive set breakfasts (**mōningu sābisu**: literally, 'morning service') and set lunches (**teishoku**) in small cafés. Cheap options for the evening meal include sandwiches, or the ubiquitous MacDonald's and Kentucky Fried Chicken.

Useful books
A short list of books which are useful sources of information in more specialist areas is to be found in the Publications section in Unit Eight, page 185.

UNIT THREE

This Unit explains how to say 'there is' and indicate where people and things are. It looks at the Japanese equivalent of 'with' (a pen, etc.), 'at' (a restaurant) and 'at' (a time). And it introduces respect language.

Structure 21: aru ('there is', etc.)

Zasshi ga arimasu.
There are magazines.
Shitsumon wa arimasu ka. Hai, futatsu arimasu.
Are there [any] questions? Yes, there are two.
Or: Do you have [any] questions? Yes, I have two.
Chokorēto ga ikutsu arimasu ka. Mittsu arimasu.
How many chocolates do you have? I have three.

CHECKNOTES 21

a) **Aru** (literally, 'exist') roughly corresponds to 'there is'/'there are' or 'has'/'have'. The appropriate translation should be clear from the context.

b) **Aru** is used only when referring to inanimate objects.

c) Before **aru** and **iru** (see Structure 22), **ga** indicates the <u>subject</u> of the sentence (not to be confused with the <u>topic</u>, indicated by **wa**).
   However, in questions and statements confirming information about a topic already known by the speakers, **wa** is used with **aru** and **iru**.

d) Note that the subject or topic of **aru** will be an object in English, if you translate **aru** as 'has'/'have'. Therefore it may be better to think of **aru** as meaning 'exist', or 'is in my, etc. possession', even though this produces rather strange English. For example, **Chizu ga arimasu** will usually be translated as 'There is a map' or 'I, etc. have a map' (where 'map' is the object of 'have' in English). But actually the meaning is nearer to 'A map exists' or 'A map is in my, etc. possession', since **chizu ga** is felt to be the subject in Japanese.

e) The basic method of counting was introduced in Structure 8. However, as noted then, different sorts of numbers, or 'counters', are used for different things. **-tsu** is the most general counter in Japanese. Although typically used to count small things such as chocolates or fruit, it tends also to be used in cases where there doesn't seem to be an appropriate counter. The forms from one to ten are irregular:

hitotsu	one	**muttsu**	six
futatsu	two	**nanatsu**	seven
mittsu	three	**yattsu**	eight
yottsu	four	**kokonotsu**	nine
itsutsu	five	**tō**	ten

Note also **ikutsu** ('how many?')

After ten, the **jū-ichi, jū-ni**, etc. system is used on its own with no counter. This latter system and most of the counters, for example, **-mai** for flat things and **-en** for Yen, originally came from Chinese. **Hitotsu, futatsu**, etc. are the remnants of the native Japanese system.

f) Note that **ga, wa, o**, etc. are not normally used after a counter.

Checklist 21

chokorēto	chocolate
inkan	seal (used instead of a signature)
kami	paper (becomes **-gami** in **ori-gami**, 'paper folding')
o-jikan	time (Polite form of **jikan**, 'time')
kippu	ticket (train, etc.)
o-kane	money
pasokon	personal computer (from **pāsonaru konpyūtā**)
shitsumon	question
sɯkoshi	(adverb) a little

FLUENCY PRACTICE 21
Translate the following sentences into English:

1 Mondai ga arimasɯ.
2 O-kane wa arimasɯ ka. Hai, sɯkoshi arimasɯ.
3 Yakɯsoku ga arimasɯ.
4 Kami wa arimasɯ ka. Hai, arimasɯ.
5 Pasokon ga arimasɯ.

Translate the following sentences into Japanese:

6 There are [some] tickets.
7 Do you have time? Yes, [I] do.
8 I have three seals.
9 Do you have a credit card? Yes, [I] have four. (Use **-mai**, not **-tsu**, as cards are flat.)
10 There is a bank.

Structure 22: iru ('there is', etc.)

Neko ga imasu.
There is a cat.
Yamaguchi-san wa imasu ka. Hai, imasu.
Is Mr/Mrs/Miss Yamaguchi [there]? Yes, he/she is.
Igirisu no Buraun-san wa imasu ka. Hai, imasu.
Is Mr Brown from the U.K. [here]? Yes, he is.

CHECKNOTES 22

a) **Iru** is similar in meaning to **aru** (Structure 21), but is used with reference to people or animals. It is often necessary to add 'in', 'here' or 'there' to make the meaning clear in English.

b) **Da** is concerned with identity; **aru** and **iru** are concerned with location (and, sometimes, possession). On occasion, all may be translated as 'be', etc. in English.

Checklist 22

annai-gakari	information officer (from **annai**, 'guide', and **kakari/gakari**, 'person in charge')
eki-in	station attendant (from **eki**, 'station', and **-in**, 'worker')
insatsu	printing
ka	mosquito
neko	cat

FLUENCY PRACTICE 22

Translate the following sentences into English:

1　Enjinia ga imasψ.
2　Ka ga imasψ.
3　Suzuki-san ga imasψ.
4　Buchō-san wa imasψ ka. Hai, imasψ.
5　Chiyoda Insatsu no Nakajima-san wa imasψ ka. Hai, imasψ.

Translate the following sentences into Japanese:

6　The station attendant is [there].
7　Is the information officer [in]? Yes, [she] is.
8　Mr Asano is [there].
9　Are the consultants [there]? Yes, [they] are.
10　Mr Jones (**Jōnzu-san**) from Jones Associates (**Jōnzu Asoshiētsu**) is [there].

Structure 23: ni (expressions of place)

Koko <u>ni</u> pen to kami ga arimasψ.
Here is a pen and [some] paper.
Kūkō <u>ni</u> annai-jo ga arimasψ.
There is an information desk <u>in</u> the airport.
Hoteru <u>ni</u> kissa-ten ga arimasψ.
There is a café <u>in</u> the hotel.
Resψtoran <u>ni</u> kōkō-sei ga imasψ.
There are [some] high school students <u>in</u> the restaurant.

CHECKNOTES 23

a)　**Ni** indicates where something or somebody is.

b)　In the same sentence, a noun with **ga** usually comes after a noun with **ni**.

Checklist 23

annai-jo	information centre/desk (**annai suru** means 'guide')
gasorin sψtando	petrol station (from 'gasoline stand')
genkan	entrance hall

hon'ya	bookshop
kissa-ten	café (literally, a 'drinking tea shop')
kōkō-sei	high school students (kōkō is short for kōtō gakkō, 'high school')
nimotsu	luggage
rōka	corridor
saifu	wallet

FLUENCY PRACTICE 23

Translate the following sentences into English:

1 Eki ni fakkɯsu ga arimasɯ.
2 Heya ni bengo-shi ga imasɯ.
3 Rōka ni denwa ga arimasɯ.
4 Genkan ni Amerika no Howaito-san (Mrs White) ga imasɯ.
5 Asoko ni gasorin sɯtando ga arimasɯ.

Translate the following sentences into Japanese:

6 There is a computer in the office.
7 There is [some] money in the wallet.
8 There are [some] consultants in the office.
9 There is a passport in the luggage.
10 Are there maps in the bookshop?

Structure 24: Negatives of aru and iru

Pan ga arimasen.
There is no bread.
Tanaka-san wa imasen.
Mr Tanaka is not in.
Sumimasen ga, kami ga arimasen.
I am sorry, but there isn't any paper.
Asoko ni wa nanimo arimasen.
There is nothing over there.
Sono kissa-ten ni wa daremo imasen.
There is nobody in that café.

CHECKNOTES 24

a) As you would expect from Structure 15, the negative forms of **arimasu** and **imasu** are **arimasen** and **imasen**, respectively.

b) **Wa** (not **ga**) is used in **Tanaka-san wa imasen**, because Mr Tanaka is known to the speakers.

c) If the place comes at the beginning of the sentence and is felt to be the topic, **ni** is followed by **wa**. For example, **Koko ni wa hon ga arimasen** ('There are no books here [but there may be somewhere else]').

d) 'Nothing' and 'nobody' are expressed by using **nanimo** and **daremo**, respectively, and a negative verb.

e) Note that in clauses with **ga** ('but'), such as **Sumimasen ga, ...** ('I'm sorry, but ...'), the comma is always after **ga**.

Checklist 24

sumimasen   I'm sorry

ga   but
hiki-dashi   drawer (from **hiku**, 'pull', and **dasu**, 'take out')
kaigi-shitsu   conference room (from **kaigi**, 'conference', and **-shitsu**, 'room')

FLUENCY PRACTICE 24

Translate the following sentences into English:

1 Hoteru ni wāpuro ga arimasen.
2 Sumimasen ga, sukiyaki ga arimasen.
3 Tsuji-san wa imasen ka.
4 Hiki-dashi ni nanimo arimasen.
5 Daremo imasen ka.

Translate the following sentences into Japanese:

6 There isn't [any] time.
7 Mr Yoshizawa is not [in].
8 I am sorry but there aren't [any] tickets.
9 There isn't anything in the room (or: There is nothing in the room). (Use **ni wa**.)
10 Nobody is in the conference room. (Use **ni wa**.)

Structure 25: de ('by', 'with', etc.)

Pen de tegami o kakimasψ.
I write letters with a pen.
Funabin/kōkūbin de kozutsumi o okurimasψ.
I send a parcel by seamail/airmail.
Nihon-go de hanashimashō.
Let's speak in Japanese.
Jidō-sha de jimu-sho ni ikimasψ.
I go to the office by car.

CHECKNOTES 25

a) De ('with', 'using', 'by', 'in') indicates the object used to do
something. It follows the noun.

Checklist 25

hanasu	speak
harau	pay
chika-tetsu	underground (from chika, 'underground', and -tetsu, 'iron')
Eigo	English (language)
fakkψsu-bun	fax message
funa-bin	seamail (from fune, 'boat', 'ship', and -bin, 'mail')
jidō-sha	car (from jidō, 'automatic', and -sha, 'vehicle')
kōkū-bin	airmail (from kōkū, 'aviation', and -bin, 'mail')
kozutsumi	parcel
Nihon-go	Japanese (language)
Nihon'en	Japanese Yen
Rimujin Basu	Limousine Bus (airport bus between Narita Airport and Tokyo)
Shinkansen	Bullet Train
takψshī	taxi

FLUENCY PRACTICE 25

Translate the following sentences into English:

1 Eigo de fakkusu-bun o kakimasu.
2 Rimujin Basu de Narita Kūkō ni ikimashō.
3 Nihon'en de kanjō o haraimashita.
4 Sumisu-shachō wa hikō-ki de kaerimashita.
5 Denwa de Nihon-go de hanashimashita.

Translate the following sentences into Japanese:

6 I wrote the report on the word processor.
7 I'm going to Ōsaka by Bullet Train.
8 Let's go by underground.
9 He made a speech in Japanese.
10 I'll go back to the hotel by taxi.

Structure 26: de ('in', 'at', etc.)

Resutoran de aimashō.
Let's meet at the restaurant.

CHECKNOTES 26

a) **De** is also used to indicate the place where an action occurs. But remember: if the verb is **aru** or **iru**, you need to use **ni** to indicate the place where the things or people are.

Checklist 26

kaeru	change (something)
okonau	hold, carry out
asa-gohan	breakfast (from **asa**, 'morning', and **gohan**, 'rice', 'meal')
hoteru no heya	hotel room
kiji	(newspaper) article
kōjō	factory
tosho-kan	library

FLUENCY PRACTICE 26

Translate the following sentences into English:

1 Watashi wa hikō-ki de hon o yomimashita.
2 Kōbe de kaigi o okonaimashita.
3 Shinbun kisha wa tosho-kan de kiji o kakimashita.
4 Kaisha no genkan de aimashō.
5 Kōjō de kikai no shashin o torimashō.

Translate the following sentences into Japanese:

6 I had (literally, 'ate') breakfast at the airport.
7 Let's talk in that café.
8 I changed [some] money at the bank.
9 Let's meet at Yoyogi station.
10 Let's watch television in the hotel room.

Structure 27: ni (expressions of time)

Nan-ji ni okimasψ ka. Shichiji ni okimasψ.
What time do you get up? I get up at 7.00.
Nan-ji ni dekakemasψ ka. Hachi-ji ni dekakemasψ.
What time do you set out? I set out at 8.00.

CHECKNOTES 27

a) **Ni** ('at') indicates the time when something happens. It is only used when specific times are involved. It is not used with some common words like **kyō** ('today') and **raishū** ('next week'). **Ni** is usually needed if numbers, such as '3 o'clock', are quoted.

Checklist 27

dekakeru	set out, leave
hajimaru	(something) begins; but **hajimeru** is used for '(somebody) begins (something)'
neru	go to bed; sleep
okiru	get up
owaru	(something) ends
tsuku	arrive
robī	lobby

torēdo fea	trade fair
itsu	when?
nan'yōbi	what day of the week?
getsu-yōbi	Monday
ka-yōbi	Tuesday
sui-yōbi	Wednesday
moku-yōbi	Thursday
kin-yōbi	Friday
do-yōbi	Saturday
nichi-yōbi	Sunday

FLUENCY PRACTICE 27

Translate the following sentences into English:

1 Nan-ji ni nemasψ ka. Jū-ichi-ji ni nemasψ.
2 Kyō wa nan'yōbi desψ ka. Sui-yōbi desψ.
3 Roku-ji ni kaisha no robī de aimashō.
4 Shichiji juppun-mae ni Haneda Kūkō ni tsukimashita.
5 Kaigi wa itsu owarimasψ ka. Go-ji ni owarimasψ.

Translate the following sentences into Japanese:

6 When does the meeting begin? It begins at 10.15.
7 When does it end? It ends at 10.45.
8 When does the trade fair begin? It begins on Tuesday.
9 What time will [you] arrive? [I]'ll arrive at 4.50.
10 The section head attended a meeting at half past four.

Structure 28: The language of respect

Japanese contains various devices to pay respect to the person or people one is talking to or about.

a) **VERBS** In addition to Polite verbs (see Structure 10), there are 'Humble' verbs and 'Honorific' verbs. Humble verbs talk down the importance of one's own actions and those in one's social group (for example, your company or family). Honorific verbs talk up the actions of those in another social group (for example, a guest, somebody from a company with which you want to do business, a teacher, somebody older).

In the case of common verbs such as 'be' and 'do', there tend to be separate verbs for the Humble and Honorific functions. For example, when the Polite style is being used, 'say' is usually **iimasy**, but the Humble verb 'say' is **mōshimasy** and the Honorific verb is **osshaimasy**.

Most verbs, however, form Humble and Honorific verbs using productive patterns.

Verbs not listed in Structures 29 and 30 can be turned into Humble and Honorific forms as follows. From now on, Humble and Honorific verbs in the Checklists will be marked 'Hum.' and 'Hon.'.

b) To make a Humble verb:
Remove the **-masu** ending. We will call the stem thus formed the **masy** stem. It is different from the verb stem (which always ends in a consonant in the case of a Consonant verb, and in a vowel in the case of a Vowel verb).
Put **o-** before, and the relevant form of **suru** after the **masy** stem. For example: **matsu** ('wait', Plain present) becomes **machimasy** (Polite present) and **o-machi shimasy** (Humble present).

c) To make an Honorific verb:
Put **o-** before, and the relevant form of **ni naru** after the **masy** stem. For example: **matsu** ('wait', Plain present) becomes **machimasy** (Polite present) and **o-machi ni narimasy** (Honorific present).

An alternative to this form of Honorific verb, particularly common among young people, is to use the passive. This is formed by adding **-areru** to the verb stem of a Consonant verb and **-rareru** to the verb stem of a Vowel verb. **Sareru** is the irregular form for **suru** ('do', 'make'). For example: **Ikaremasy ka** ('Are you going?').

d) **OTHER PARTS OF SPEECH** The concepts of Polite, Humble and Honorific are applied not just to verbs, but also to nouns, pronouns, adjectives and adverbs. The prefixes **o-** and **go-** often make nouns Honorific, for example: **shigoto** ('my work') but **o-shigoto** ('your work'); **benkyō** ('my studies') but **go-benkyō** ('your studies').

There is a system for forming Humble adjectives, but it is rarely used and beyond the scope of this book. The approach to these concepts throughout the rest of the language is more piecemeal. We will mark such items as they come up, 'Pol.', 'Hum.' or 'Hon.'. For example: **kanai** (Hum. 'my, etc. wife'); **okฺusan** (Hon. 'your, etc. wife').

Structure 29: Common Honorific verbs

Shachō-sama wa irasshaimasฺ ka.
Is the company president in?
Kyōto ni irasshaimasฺ ka.
Are you going to Kyoto?
O-sake de mo meshiagarimasen ka.
Won't you drink some rice wine or something?

CHECKNOTES 29
a) Here are some common Honorific verbs:

da	*de irasshaimasฺ	be
iru	irasshaimasฺ	exist
iku	irasshaimasฺ	go
kuru	irasshaimasฺ	come
suru	nasaimasฺ	do, make
yuu	osshaimasฺ	say
taberu	meshiagarimasฺ	eat
nomu	meshiagarimasฺ	drink
miru	goran ni narimasฺ	see
kureru	kudasaimasฺ	give

*Only used when a person is the subject.

b) All the above Honorific verbs have been given in the Polite present, as this is much more common than the Plain present in the case of Honorific verbs.

However, note that the Plain forms of **de irasshaimasฺ**, **irasshaimasฺ**, **nasaimasฺ**, **osshaimasฺ** and **kudasaimasฺ** are **de irassharu, irassharu, nasaru, ossharu** and **kudasaru**. For some reason, the 'r' drops out in all of the Polite forms.

Checklist 29

benkyō suru	study
kureru	(somebody equal or superior) gives (me, etc.)
yuu	say; all other forms are as if the Plain present were 'iu'; Polite present **iimasψ**, etc.
de mo	or something (follows noun)
dochira	Pol. of **doko**, 'where?'
fuku-buchō	deputy manager
Makuhari Messe	Makuhari Trade Fair ('Messe' from German)
o-kyakψ-sama	Hon. of **o-kyakψ-san**, 'guest', 'customer' (no distinction in Japanese!)
-sama	more polite than **-san**, 'Mr', 'Mrs', 'Miss'
Shitsurei desu ga,...	Excuse me, but ...
sō yuu	say so

FLUENCY PRACTICE 29

Translate the following sentences into English:

1 Shitsurei desu ga, Igirisu no Pψritchādo-sama (Miss Pritchard) de irasshaimasψ ka.
2 Okazaki-sensei wa sō osshaimashɨta.
3 Dochira de Nihon-go o benkyō nasaimashɨta ka.
4 Yokohama Kikai no Takeuchi-sama ga irasshaimasψ.
5 Sψki-yaki de mo meshiagarimasen ka.

Translate the following sentences into Japanese, using Honorific forms where appropriate:

6 Are there any customers?
7 The deputy manager is in the conference room.
8 Are [you] going to the Makuhari Trade Fair?
9 Is the company president [in]?
10 Won't [you] watch the television?

Structure 30: Common Humble verbs

Kōkan-shu:	**Fujisawa Kagaku de gozaimasɯ.**
Reception:	This is Fujisawa Chemicals.
Deibiddo Sɯmisu:	**Sōmu-ka no Katō-san o-negai shimasɯ.**
David Smith:	Mr Kato in the general affairs section, please.
Kōkan-shu:	**Sōmu-ka no Katō de gozaimasu ne. Shōshō o-machi kudasai.**
Reception:	Mr Kato in the general affairs section? Please wait a moment.

Sochira de gozaimasɯ.
It's there.
Yoroshɨku o-negai itashimasɯ.
Pleased to meet you.
Kore kara mo yoroshɨku o-negai shimasɯ.
I'll look forward to your helping me from now on.

CHECKNOTES 30

a) Here are some common Humble verbs:

da	de gozaimasɯ	be
aru	gozaimasɯ	exist
iru	orimasɯ	exist
iku	mairimasɯ	go
kuru	mairimasɯ	come
suru	itashimasɯ	do
miru	haiken shimasɯ	see
yomu	haiken shimasɯ	read
kariru	haishaku shimasɯ	borrow
yuu	mōshimasɯ	say
omou	zonjimasɯ	think
tazuneru	ukagaimasɯ	visit
kiku	ukagaimasɯ	hear; ask
ageru	sashi-agemasɯ	give
morau	itadakimasɯ	receive

b) **Ne** at the end of a sentence, as in **Sōmu-ka no Katō de gozaimasu ne** ('[It]'s Mr Kato in the general affairs section [you want], isn't it?'), adds the sense of 'isn't it?', 'doesn't it?', etc., like 'n'est-ce pas?' in French. Sometimes it just indicates that the speaker is seeking the agreement of the person listening, in which case it is difficult to translate into English.

c) **Shōsho o-machi kudasai** ('Please wait a moment') is more polite than **Chotto matte kudasai**. See Structure 34.

d) **Sochira de gozaimasu** ('It's there') is more polite than **Soko desu**.

e) **Yoroshiku o-negai itashimasu** ('Pleased to meet you') is the Humble form of **Yoroshiku o-negai shimasu**. The same expression is also used when asking a favour: for example, **Kore kara mo yoroshiku o-negai shimasu** ('I'll look forward to your helping me from now on'). This sounds presumptuous in English, but is normal in Japanese as it recognizes the superior position of the other person.

f) Floors are counted in **-kai**, but there are several irregular forms.

nangai	what floor?	**rokkai**	sixth floor
ikkai	first floor	**hakkai**	eighth floor
sangai	third floor	**jukkai (jikkai)**	tenth floor

The Japanese refer to the ground floor as **ikkai**, the first floor as **ni-kai**, etc.

Checklist 30

ageru	give (to an equal or superior)
mairu	Consonant verb; Hum. of **iku**, 'go', and **kuru**, 'come'
oru	Hum. of **iru**, 'exist' (of living things)
sashi-ageru	Hum. of **ageru**
achira	Pol. of **are**, 'that (one over there)', or **asoko**, 'over there'
kochira	Pol. of **kore**, 'this (one)', or **koko**, 'here'
sochira	Pol. of **sore**, 'that (one) (already mentioned)', or **soko**, 'there'
isu	chair

kagaku   chemistry; in company names, 'Chemicals'
kyonen   last year
sōmu-ka   general affairs section
watakⱷshi   Hum. of **watashi**, 'I', 'me'

FLUENCY PRACTICE 30

Translate the following sentences into English:

1 Otearai wa achira de gozaimasⱷ.
2 Sore de wa, asatte ukagaimasⱷ.
3 Kaigi-shitsu wa ni-kai de gozaimasⱷ.
4 Sochira ni isu ga gozaimasⱷ. Dōzo o-kake kudasai.
5 Hakata ni shutchō itashimasⱷ.

Translate the following sentences into Japanese, using Humble forms where appropriate:

6 I am called Jones (**Jōnzu**).
7 I'm going to Ōsaka tomorrow.
8 There is a telephone over there.
9 [Our] company president went to Japan last year.
10 I read [your] (**Okazaki-san no**) report, Mr Okazaki.

CONVERSATION 6: Mōningu sābisu
('Breakfast in a café')

Wētoresu: Irasshaimase. Go-chūmon wa nan ni nasaimasɰ ka.
Deibiddo Sɰmisu: Mōningu sābisu o o-negai shimasɰ.
Wētoresu: Mōningu sābisu ni wa setto A (ē), setto B (bī), setto C (shī) to gozaimasɰ. Setto A wa piza tōsɰto, kɰrowassan, yoguruto, kōhī to orenji jūsu de, setto B wa tōsɰto, sɰkɰranburudo eggu, bēkon, kōhī to orenji jūsu de, setto C wa gohan, miso-shiru, medama-yaki, tsuke-mono to ni-mono de gozaimasɰ.
Deibiddo Sɰmisu: De wa setto A o o-negai shimasɰ.
Wētoresu: O-matase itashimashɨta. A setto de gozaimasɰ.
Deibiddo Sɰmisu: *(When he has finished his meal)* O-kanjō o o-negai shimasɰ.

Waitress: Hello. What would you like to order?
David Smith: I'd like a set breakfast please.
Waitress: There are Set A, Set B and Set C for set breakfast. Set A is pizza toast, croissant, yoghurt, coffee and orange juice. Set B is toast, scrambled egg, bacon, coffee and orange juice. Set C is rice, miso soup, fried egg, pickles and ni-mono.
David Smith: In that case, I'll have Set A, please.
Waitress: Sorry for keeping you waiting. Here's your Set A.
David Smith: Could I have the bill, please?

Notes on Conversation 6

a) **Mōningu sābisu** (literally, 'morning service') refers to a reasonably priced menu of breakfasts, available in cafés, etc.

b) **To (gozaimasɰ)** indicates that the last item in a series has been mentioned.

c) **O-matase itashimashɨta** is the Humble form of **O-matase shimashɨta** ('I kept you waiting').

d) New words:

bēkon	bacon
de wa = sore de wa	in that case
gohan	rice
kψrowassan	croissant
medama-yaki	fried egg
miso-shiru	miso soup
ni-mono	Japanese-style boiled food
piza tōsψto	pizza on a toast base. **Tōsψto** may be as much as an inch thick!
sψkψranburudo eggu	scrambled egg

CONVERSATION 7: Hoteru no resepψshon nite: Tsūrisψto infomēshon wa doko desψ ka
('At the hotel reception: Where is the tourist information centre?')

Deibiddo Sψmisu: Sumimasen. Kono chikaku ni tsūrisψto infomēshon wa arimasψ ka.

Uketsuke no hito: Kono hoteru no robī ni, kaigai kara no o-kyakψ-sama no tame no desψku ga gozaimasψ.

Deibiddo Sψmisu: Dōmo arigatō.

David Smith: *Excuse me. Is there a tourist information centre near here?*

Person at desk: *There is a desk for visitors from abroad in the lobby of this hotel.*

David Smith: *Thank you.*

Notes on Conversation 7

a) **Kaigai kara** means 'from abroad' and **o-kyakψ-sama** means 'guests'. **Kaigai kara** is describing **o-kyakψ-sama**, so a **no** is needed to link the two. Similarly, **no** is needed to link (**o-kyakψ-sama no) tame** and **desψku**. If two nouns stand together without **no**, they are nearly always a compound noun, for example: **denwa bangō** ('phone number').

b) **No tame no** means literally 'for the purpose or benefit of ...'. It follows the noun.

c) New words:

desγ̵ku	desk
dōmo arigatō	thank you, more polite than **dōmo**
kaigai	abroad
kono chikaku	near here (literally, 'this neighbourhood')
tsūrisγ̵to infomēshon	tourist information (centre)

CONVERSATION 8: Kōhī de mo meshiagarimasen ka ('Would you like a coffee or something?')

Toyoda: Kōhī de mo meshiagarimasen ka.
Deibiddo Sγ̵misu: Ē, itadakimasγ̵.

Toyoda: Would you like a coffee or something?
David Smith: Yes, please.

Notes on Conversation 8

a) **Ē, itadakimasγ̵** (literally, 'Yes, I will receive', Hum.) is a politer way of accepting something than **o-negai shīmasγ̵**.

CONVERSATION 9: Shinkansen no kippu o kau ('Buying a Bullet Train ticket')

Deibiddo Sγ̵misu: Nagoya made kata-michi o ichi-mai o-negai shimasγ̵.
Mado-guchi no hito: Shitei-seki desγ̵ ka, jiyū-seki desγ̵ ka.
Deibiddo Sγ̵misu: Shitei-seki de o-negai shimasγ̵.
Mado-guchi no hito: Tsugi no Nagoya-yuki wa 15(jū-go)-ji 25(ni-jū-go)-fun ni narimasu ga, yoroshii desγ̵ ka.
Deibiddo Sγ̵misu: Hai.
Mado-guchi no hito: Kin'en-seki desγ̵ ka, kitsuen-seki desγ̵ ka.
Deibiddo Sγ̵misu: Kin'en-seki de o-negai shimasγ̵.

David Smith: Single to Nagoya, please.
Person in booth: Do you want a reserved seat or a free seat?
David Smith: A reserved seat, please.

Person in booth: *The next train to Nagoya is at 15:25. Is that all right?*
David Smith: *Yes.*
Person in booth: *Do you want a non-smoking seat or a smoking seat?*
David Smith: *Non-smoking, please.*

Notes on Conversation 9

a) **Shitei-seki desu̶ ka, jiyū-seki desu̶ ka** means literally, 'Is it a reserved seat, is it a free seat (that you want)?' Note that, in Japanese, you ask two questions 'Is it A? Is it B?', rather than saying 'Is it A or B?' when offering an alternative.

b) In **Shitei-seki de o-negai shimasu̶** the **de** indicates that you will be travelling in a reserved seat (see Structure 26).

c) **-yuki** is a suffix meaning 'train to ...'.

d) New words:

jiyū-seki	free seat (from **jiyū da**, 'free', and **zaseki**, 'seat')
kata-michi	one-way ticket
kin'en-seki	non-smoking seat
kitsuen-seki	smoking seat
naru	(preceded by **ni**) is at (literally, 'becomes')
shitei-seki	reserved seat
tsugi	next (takes **no** if followed by noun)
yoroshii	all right (Polite form of **ii**, 'good')

INFORMATION: On arrival in Japan

Language
Although most Japanese study English for many years at school, few have frequent opportunities to use it. It is therefore unwise to assume that you will be able to communicate in English at all times. However, airport officials and staff in major hotels will almost certainly speak English: mercifully, there is no need to force your jet-lagged brain to struggle with the intricacies of the Japanese language after a long-haul flight.

Telephones
It is possible to phone the U.K. using a telephone card (or many ¥100 coins!) from special international telephone boxes (usually bright green). It is also possible to make calls using a credit card from a limited number of public telephones.

Japan is 9 hours ahead of G.M.T. (and therefore 8 hours ahead during British summer time).

Telephone cards (known as **terehon kādo**) are sold by machines near public telephones. They tend to work out cheaper than using coins, and are generally more convenient. Since telephoning in a foreign language is always slightly stressful, anything which makes life easier is probably a good thing! Japanese telephone cards are much thinner than British ones and come in a variety of attractive designs. You can have personalized ones made which make excellent small presents.

Taxi vouchers
You may well be given a taxi voucher during the course of your business calls. This is a voucher to be given to a taxi driver who will then charge whomever (or whichever institution) gave you the voucher.

Crossing the road
The Japanese drive on the left-hand side, but traffic rules seem a little different from in the U.K.: there are times when cars may still cross the pedestrian crossing, even if the pedestrians have a green light.

Electricity
Mains voltage in Japan is 100v a.c., although shaver sockets often also provide 220v a.c. Small, two-pinned plugs are used.

UNIT FOUR

Now we learn how to say 'and', 'before', 'after' and 'so'; how to
describe continuous actions and indicate the results of an action;
how to ask people to do things for you; and how to express ability.
We also look at the Plain past.

Structure 31: (verb)-te (linking sentences)

Depāto ni itte, kaimono shimashita.
I went to the department store and did the shopping.
Kuroda-san ni denwa or kakete, yakusoku o shimashita.
I phoned Mr Kuroda and made an appointment.

CHECKNOTES 31

a) The -te form of a verb has various uses. One of the most
common is to link two sentences. In this use, it often translates
as 'and' in English. The -te form does not change for tense, so
it may be translated by a present, future or past verb,
according to context, in English.

b) To make the -te form, remove masu and add te to the
remaining stem. Note that, over the centuries, various sound
changes have occurred:

No change:

hanaS.u ('speak')	hanaSH.i.masu	becomes hanaSH.i.te
tabE.ru ('eat')	tabE.masu	becomes tabE.te
mi.ru ('see')	mi.masu	becomes mi.te

CH.i.te, (W).i.te, R.i.te change to tte:

maTS.u ('wait')	maCH.i.masu	becomes matte
wara(W).u ('laugh')	wara(W).i.masu	becomes waratte
okuR.u ('send')	okuR.i.masu	becomes okutte

G.i.te changes to ide:

oyoG.u ('swim')	oyoG.i.masu	becomes oyoide

ki-te changes to ite:

kaku ('write')	kaK.i.masu	becomes kaite

73

B.i.te, M.i.te, N.i.te change to **nde**:

yo**B**.u ('call')	yo**B.i**.mas**ɰ**	becomes **yonde**
yo**M**.u ('read')	yo**M.i**.mas**ɰ**	becomes **yonde**
shi**N**.u ('die')	shi**N.i**.mas**ɰ**	becomes **shinde**

Irregular:

da ('be')	des**ɰ**	becomes **de**
iku ('go')	i**K.i**.mas**ɰ**	becomes **itte**
suru ('do')	sh**i**.mas**ɰ**	becomes **shi.te**
kuru ('come')	k**i**.mas**ɰ**	becomes **ki.te**

c) The verbs **hairu** ('enter') (Consonant verb) and **noru** ('get on'), which you will meet in the Fluency Practice sentences, take **ni** where one might have expected **o**. For example: **heya ni hairu** ('enter a room') and **densha ni noru** ('get on a train').

Checklist 31

kaette kuru	come back (from **kaeru**, 'return', and **kuru**, 'come')
kaimono suru	do the shopping (from **kau**, 'buy', and **mono**, 'thing')
kakunin suru	confirm
nakɰ**su**	lose
yakɰ**soku o suru**	make an appointment

e-hagaki	picture postcard (from **e**, 'picture', and **hagaki**, 'postcard')
kitte	stamp
mise	shop (from **miseru**, 'show')
omiyage	souvenir
taishi-kan	embassy; **Igirisu Taishi-kan** the British Embassy
terehon kādo	telephone card
yoyaku	reservation

FLUENCY PRACTICE 31

Translate the following sentences into English:

1 Asakusa ni itte, omiyage o kaimashita.
2 Yokohama e itte, Nissan no Suzuki-san ni aimashita.
3 Watashi wa ashita Shizuoka ni itte, asatte kaette kimasu.
4 Genkan ni haitte, denwa o kakemashita.
5 Chika-tetsu ni notte, hoteru ni kaerimashita.

Translate the following sentences into Japanese:

6 I went to the shop and bought a telephone card.
7 I bought the stamps and sent the postcard.
8 I phoned and confirmed the hotel reservation.
9 I used the database and collected the information (use **shiryō**).
10 I lost my passport and went to the British Embassy.

Structure 32: (verb)-te iru (continuous actions)

Satō-san wa nani o <u>shite imasu</u> ka.
What <u>is</u> Mr Satō <u>doing</u>?
Andō-kachō wa ima <u>shigoto o shite imasu</u>.
Mr Andō, the section head, <u>is working</u> now.
Ikebukuro ni <u>sunde imasu</u>.
I <u>am living</u> in Ikebukuro.

CHECKNOTES 32

a) The (verb)-**te iru** structure has two main usages. The first is to express continuous action: 'be (verb)-ing'. The other main usage is dealt with in Structure 33.

b) Like **aru** and **iru**, **sumu** ('live') takes **ni**, not **de**, to indicate place.

Checklist 32

sagasu	look for
anyuaru repōto = nenpō	annual report
kachō	section head
tori-hiki	dealings; **tori-hiki o suru** trade

FLUENCY PRACTICE 32

Translate the following sentences into English:

1 Kanojo wa ganbatte imasɯ.
2 Kare wa ima denwa o kakete imasɯ.
3 Itō-buchō (Mr Itoh, the department head) wa Tōkyō de
tori-hiki o shite imasɯ.
4 Sumimasen ga, Roiyaru Fānichā no Eigo no anyuaru repōto
o sagashite imasɯ.
5 Ima Rondon ni sunde imasɯ.

Translate the following sentences into Japanese:

6 Mr Saitō is reading the newspaper.
7 She's writing a report today.
8 Mr Andō is working in the factory in Kobe (use **Kōbe no
kōjō**).
9 The section head is having (literally, 'eating') [his] lunch now.
10 The reporter was writing an article.

Structure 33: (verb)-te iru (results of an action)

Konpyūtā ga <u>koshō shite imasɯ</u>.
The computer <u>is broken</u>/<u>has broken down</u>.
Denki ga <u>tsuite/kiete imasɯ</u>.
The light <u>is on</u>/<u>off</u>.
Poketto ni kagi ga <u>haitte imasɯ</u>.
<u>There is</u> a key in the pocket.
<u>Komatte imasɯ</u>.
<u>I'm in a fix</u>.

CHECKNOTES 33

a) In addition to the use explained in Structure 32, (verb)-**te iru** is
used to indicate states which are the result of some action. In
English, it is sometimes equivalent to an adjective and
sometimes to a verb in the perfect tense.

b) Note that the subject is usually marked by **ga** in this structure.
But if the subject is something or somebody known to the
speakers, i.e. a topic, it is indicated by **wa**.

Checklist 33

aku	(something) opens
gaishutsu suru	go out
haitte iru	have entered, be (put) (from **hairu**, 'enter'); 'in' is **ni**
kekkon suru	get married
kieru	go out (of electrical device)
komaru	be in a fix; be a nuisance
komu	crowd
koshō suru	break down
kowareru	(something) breaks
shimaru	(something) closes
tsukareru	get tired
tsuku	come on (of electrical device)
hontō ni	really (from **hontō (no)**, 'true')
mada	still, yet
denki	electricity; **denki ga tsuku** a light comes on; **denki ga kieru** a light goes out
doa	door
dokμshin	single (person)
kabin	vase
michi	road

FLUENCY PRACTICE 33
Translate the following sentences into English:

1 Hontō ni tsukarete imasμ.
2 Doa ga aite imasμ.
3 Kachō wa gaishutsu shite imasμ.
4 Densha wa mada kite imasen.
5 Kare wa kekkon shite imasμ ka.

Translate the following sentences into Japanese:

6 Are [you] married? No, I'm still single (literally, 'single person').
7 This window is shut.
8 The light is off.
9 This road is crowded.
10 The vase is broken.

Structure 34: (verb)-te kudasai ('please ...')

Nihon-go de tegami o kaite kudasai.
Please write the letter in Japanese.
Sō shite kudasaimasen ka.
Wouldn't you do that for me?

CHECKNOTES 34

a) (Verb)-**te kudasai** means 'Please (verb)'.

b) The negative **-masen ka** ('won't you?' – see Structure 15) is also used as a slightly politer form: (verb)-**te kudasaimasen ka**.

Checklist 34

hon'yaku suru	translate; 'into' is **ni**
honbu	main branch (of a company)
keiyaku	contract
shōsai	details
yoku	well
yukkuri	slowly

FLUENCY PRACTICE 34

Translate the following sentences into English:

1 Asatte denwa o kakete kudasai.
2 Yoshioka-san ni fakk╨su o okutte kudasai.
3 Chotto matte kudasai.
4 Kore o Eigo ni hon'yaku shite kudasaimasen ka.
5 Shachō no setsumei o yoku kiite kudasai.

Translate the following sentences into Japanese:

6 Please speak in English.
7 Please take a photo. (Use **-te kudasaimasen ka**.)
8 Please read the contract well.
9 Please send the details by fax (... **o** ... **de**).
10 Please send this parcel to the main branch (... **o** ... **ni**).

Structure 35: (verb)-te kara ('after ...-ing')

Ueno eki ni itte kara, kippu o kaimashita.
After going to Ueno station, I bought the tickets.
Kūkō de chekku in shite kara, kissa-ten de kōhī o nomimashita.
After checking in at the airport, we had a coffee in a café.

CHECKNOTES 35
a) (Verb)-**te kara** gives the sense of 'after doing' something.

Checklist 35

to	with (follows the noun)
chekku in suru	check in
shiraberu	look up, check; **jisho de shiraberu** look up in a dictionary
sōdan suru	discuss
sotsugyō suru	graduate
bā	bar
ban-gohan	dinner (from **ban**, 'evening', and **gohan**, 'rice', 'meal')
jikoku-hyō	timetable
jisho	dictionary
kabu	share, stock
kanarazu	without fail, definitely
keikaku	plan
uchi	home

FLUENCY PRACTICE 35
Translate the following sentences into English:

1 Igirisu ni kaette kara, kanarazu tegami o kakimasu.
2 Sotsugyō shite kara, Nihon ni ikimashita.
3 Ban-gohan o tabete kara, bā ni ikimashita.
4 Keikaku o mite kara, Yoshida-san to sōdan shimasu.
5 Jikoku-hyō de densha o shirabete kara, kippu o kaimashita.

Translate the following sentences into Japanese:

6 After drinking the coffee, he read the newspaper.
7 After reading the annual report of the company, I bought the shares.
8 After sending the fax, she went home.
9 We looked for a hotel after arriving in Nagoya.
10 I set out after (eating) breakfast.

Structure 36: (verb)-u mae ni ('before ...-ing')

Nihon ni <u>iku mae ni</u>, shiryō o atsumemashita.
I collected the information <u>before going</u> to Japan.
Keiyaku o <u>musubu mae ni</u>, naiyō o kakunin shimashō.
Let's confirm the contents <u>before entering into</u> the contract.

CHECKNOTES 36
a) (Verb)-**u mae ni** means 'before doing' something. This structure consists of the Plain present of a verb followed by **mae ni**.

Checklist 36

musubu	tie; **keiyaku o musubu** enter into a contract
kawase-ritsu	exchange rate
manyuaru	manual
mazu	first
naiyō	contents

FLUENCY PRACTICE 36
Translate the following sentences into English:

1 Konpyūtā o tsukau mae ni, mazu manyuaru o yomimashita.
2 Himeno-san ni au mae ni, ginkō ni ikimasu.
3 Kaigi ni deru mae ni, denwa o kakemashita.
4 Igirisu ni kaeru mae ni, hikō-ki o kakunin shite kudasai.
5 Kurejitto kādo o tsukau mae ni, kawase-ritsu o shirabemashō.

Translate the following sentences into Japanese:

6   We bought the Japanese Yen before going to Japan.
7   Please pay the bill before [you] go.
8   I read the annual report before meeting the president.
9   Please confirm the hotel reservation before going to Japan.
10 Before I go back to Britain, let's have a drink. (Use **ga** after **watashi**, not **wa**, as clauses with **mae ni** count as relative clauses – see Structure 61.)

Structure 37: kara ('so', 'because')

Wakarimasen kara, mō ichido itte kudasai.
I don't understand, so please say it again.
Nihon-go wa dekimasen kara, tsūyaku o sagashite imasu.
I can't speak Japanese, so I'm looking for an interpreter.
Mō jikan desu kara, sorosoro kaerimashō.
Since it's already time, let's go home.

CHECKNOTES 37

a) Putting **kara** at the end of the first of two clauses adds the idea of 'so'. This can also be pressed into service for 'because', 'since' and 'as'. The translation of the second example above could be 'I'm looking for an interpreter because I can't speak Japanese'.

b) Note that, in the second example above, **Nihon-go** ('Japanese') is the topic of the sentence. It is as if the Japanese say 'Japanese? I can't speak it'.

c) (Verb)-**te miru** means '(verb) and see' or 'try (verb)-ing': **Akai botan o oshite mimashō** ('Let's try pushing the red button'). It is uncertain whether the action results in success.

Checklist 37

dasu	take out; post, send (a letter); hand in
dekiru	be able (to speak)
osu	push
shitsurei suru	be rude; say goodbye, leave
unten suru	drive

akai	red
bejitarian	vegetarian
botan	button
kesa	this morning
kuruma	car
mō ichi-do	again (literally, 'one more time')
o-niku	meat
o-saki ni	before you, etc.
totemo	very
tsūyaku	interpreter

FLUENCY PRACTICE 37

Translate the following sentences into English:

1 Tsukarete imashita kara, sugu yasumimashita.
2 Shigoto ga owarimashita kara, o-saki ni shitsurei shimasɰ.
3 Nan de mo ii desɰ (idiom meaning 'it doesn't matter what') kara, itte mite kudasai.
4 Isoide (i)masɰ kara, sugu repōto o dashite kudasai. (Note that the 'i' of -**te** (or -**de**) **iru** is commonly dropped here and elsewhere in colloquial speech.)
5 O-sake o nomimashita kara, kuruma o unten shimasen.

Translate the following sentences into Japanese:

6 I'm a vegetarian, so I don't eat meat. (Use 'contrasting' **wa** in the second clause, not **o**, to hint that you do eat other things.)
7 I'm very tired because I arrived in Japan this morning. (Use **tsuita** <u>bakari</u> desɰ, 'have <u>just</u> arrived'.)
8 He doesn't understand Japanese, so let's speak English.
9 We have time, so let's go into a café and have (drink) a (Japanese) tea or something.
10 The (company) president is not in (use **oru**, rather than **iru**, as he belongs to your humble company) now, so please wait a moment (use **o-machi kudasai**).

Structure 38: (verb)-u + koto ga dekiru (expressing ability)

Nihon-go de denwa o kakeru <u>koto ga dekimasu</u> ka.   <u>Can</u> you make a phone call in Japanese?   **Nihon-go wa <u>dekimasu</u> ka.**   <u>Can</u> you <u>speak</u> Japanese?

CHECKNOTES 38

a) The Plain present of a verb plus **koto ga dekiru** expresses ability, 'can'.

b) Sometimes, especially with **hanasu** ('speak'), (Plain present) **koto ga** is omitted. For example, 'Can you speak English?' is **Eigo wa dekimasu ka** (rather than **Eigo wa hanasu koto ga dekimasu ka**).

   Verbs ending in **suru** – for example, **yushutsu suru** ('export') – usually omit **suru koto ga**. So 'be able to export' is **yushutsu dekiru**.

Checklist 38

kotaeru	answer; **shitsumon <u>ni</u> kotaeru** answer a question
chokusetsu	directly
den'atsu	voltage
made ni	by (a deadline) (follows noun)
yūbin-kyoku	post office

FLUENCY PRACTICE 38

Translate the following sentences into English:

1 Koko de chiketto o kau koto ga dekimasu ka.

2 Raishū no moku-yōbi made ni shōsai o kakunin (suru koto ga) dekimasu ka.

3 Den'atsu no mondai ga arimasu kara, Nihon de kono kikai o tsukau koto ga dekimasen.

4 Kaikei-shi wa sono shitsumon ni kotaeru koto ga dekimasen.

5 Katō-san no hisho wa wāpuro o tsukau koto ga dekimasen.

Translate the following sentences into Japanese:

6 Can [you] play golf?
7 The lawyer can explain those problems.
8 Can [I] send a fax from the post office?
9 Can [you] go directly to Nagoya?
10 [My] wife was ill (use **byōki deshita**), so she couldn't go to the party.

Structure 39: The Plain past

Pari de Nihon-go o <u>naratta</u>.
I <u>learnt</u> Japanese in Paris.
Kyōto kara Nagoya made basu de <u>itta</u>.
I, etc. <u>went</u> from Kyoto to Nagoya by bus.
Ano hi wa ii tenki <u>datta</u>?
<u>Was</u> it good weather that day?

CHECKNOTES 39

a) The Plain past of a verb is formed by changing the final 'e' of the **-te** form to 'a'.

b) **Da** has the irregular form **datta**.

c) Note that **ka** is usually omitted when asking a question in the Plain style. Instead, use a rising, question intonation. A parallel in English would be the intonation used in 'Understand?' as opposed to 'Do you understand?'

d) The Plain past is used in idioms such as the following:

Komatta!   What a nuisance! (Literally, 'I have got in a fix!')
Shimatta!   Bother!
Bikkuri shita! You/It surprised me! (The surprise is almost always unpleasant!)

Checklist 39

bikkuri suru   be surprised
narau   learn

atarashii   new

ban	evening; **kinō no ban** yesterday evening
bangumi	(television, etc.) programme
hi	day; sun; fire
kazoku	(my, etc.) family
kudamono	fruit
no tame ni	for (literally, 'for the benefit of')
omoshiroi	interesting
ototoi	the day before yesterday
purezento	present
senshū	last week
tenki	weather

FLUENCY PRACTICE 39

Translate the following sentences into English:

1 Asa-gohan o tabeta.
2 Kyonen Rondon ni itta.
3 Kinō no ban terebi de omoshiroi bangumi o mita.
4 Kare-ra wa atarashii konpyūtā o katta.
5 Kono hon o yonda?

Translate the following sentences into Japanese using Plain forms:

6 The lawyer read the contract.
7 I bought a present for [my] family.
8 I arrived in Japan the day before yesterday.
9 Did [you] buy some fruit?
10 Did [you] meet Mr Yamaguchi last week?

CONVERSATION 10: **Hoteru no resepɰshon nite: Watashi-ate ni messēji wa haitte imasen ka.**
('At the hotel reception: Have any messages come in for me?')

Deibiddo Sɰmisu: 1012(Ichi zero ichi ni)-gōshitsu no Deibiddo Sɰmisu desu ga, nanika messēji wa haitte imasen ka.

Uketsuke no hito: Hai, ikken haitte orimasɰ. Dōzo kochira de gozaimasɰ.

Deibiddo Sɰmisu: Arigatō.

David Smith: *I'm David Smith from room 1012. Are there any messages for me?*
Receptionist: *Yes, there is one for you. Here it is.*
David Smith: *Thank you.*

Notes on Conversation 10

a) In **Nanika messēji wa haitte imasen ka** ('Have any messages come in for me?'), **nanika** ('something') is used to make the statement vaguer (and, therefore, politer). Negative questions ending in **-masen ka**, etc. are often more polite than questions ending in **-masɰ ka**. **Haitte imasɰ** means 'have come in' (see Structure 33) rather than 'are coming in'.

b) **-ken** is a counter for messages. Note: 1 **ikken**; 6 **rokken**; 8 **hakken**; and 10 **jukken** (or **jikken**).

c) **Haitte oru** is Hum. for **haitte iru**.

d) New words:

arigatō	thank you (not as polite as **dōmo arigatō**)
-ate ni	for (somebody; used of letters, etc.)
dōzo	please; here you are (like 'bitte' in German)
messēji	message

CONVERSATION 11: Hōmon jikan no kakunin
('Confirming the time of a visit')

Kōkan-shu: Nanbu Depāto de gozaimasψ.
Deibiddo Sψmisu: Eigyō 3(san)-ka no Suzuki-san o o-negai
shimasψ.
Kōkan-shu: Eigyō 3-ka no Suzuki desu ne, shōshō
o-machi kudasai.
Suzuki: Hai, Suzuki de gozaimasψ.
Deibiddo Sψmisu: Moshimoshi, Roiyaru Fānichā no Deibiddo
Sψmisu desψ.
Suzuki: Dōmo o-sewa ni natte orimasψ.
Deibiddo Sψmisu: Senjitsu o-tegami de o-negai itashimashɨta yō
ni, ashɨta 10(jū)-ji ni o-ukagai shimasu ga,
yoroshii deshō·ka.
Suzuki: Hai, o-machi itashɨte orimasψ.
Deibiddo Sψmisu: De wa, ashɨta 10-ji ni o-ukagai shimasψ.

Switchboard: Nanbu Department Store.
David Smith: Mr Suzuki in the 3rd sales section, please.
Switchboard: Mr Suzuki in the 3rd sales section? Please
wait a moment.
Suzuki: Suzuki, here.
David Smith: Hello, it's David Smith from Royal Furniture.
Suzuki: You've been very helpful to me recently [set
phrase; used more widely in Japanese].
David Smith: As I mentioned in my letter the other day, I'm
coming to see you at ten o'clock tomorrow. Is
that all right?
Suzuki: Yes. I'll be expecting you.
David Smith: I'll come at ten o'clock then.

Notes on Conversation 11

a) Note that -san is not used by the operator of somebody in
his/her own humble company, or, of course, by Suzuki referring
to himself.

b) **Dōmo o-sewa ni natte orimasψ** is the Humble form of
O-sewa ni natte imasψ, a set phrase meaning 'Thank you for
all your help'. **Dōmo** just adds a little emphasis here.

c) **Yō ni** means 'as', but comes at the end of the Japanese clause, for example: **senjitsu o-tegami de o-negai itashimashi̇ta yō ni** ('as I requested in my recent letter').

d) **O-ukagai suru** ('visit') is the Humble form of **ukagau**, which, in turn, is the Humble form of **tazuneru** ('visit'; 'ask').

e) For **Yoroshii deshō ka** ('Would that be all right?'), see Structure 49. **Yoroshii** is politer than **ii** ('good').

f) **O-machi itashite orimasɯ** ('I'll be waiting [for you]') is the Humble form of **O-machi shi̇te orimasɯ**, Hum. of **O-machi shi̇te imasɯ**, which in turn is Hum. of **Matte imasɯ**!

g) New words:

eigyō 3(san)-ka	3rd sales section
hōmon	visit
kōkan-shu	operator (from **kōkan**, 'exchange')
moshimoshi	hello (usually only used on the telephone)
o-tegami	letter (Hon. for **tegami**)

CONVERSATION 12: Aite ga fuzai no bāi
('When the person you are calling is out')

Kōkan-shu: Nanbu Depāto de gozaimasɯ.

Deibiddo Sɯmisu: Eigyō 3(san)-ka no Suzuki-san o o-negai shimasɯ.

Kōkan-shu: Shibaraku o-machi kudasai.

Dōryō: O-denwa kawarimashi̇ta. Ainiku Suzuki wa gaishutsu shi̇te orimasu ga ...

Deibiddo Sɯmisu: Nan-ji ni modoraremasɯ ka.

Dōryō: 3(San)-ji ni modoru yotei desɯ.

Deibiddo Sɯmisu: Sore de wa, 3-ji ni mō ichi-do o-denwa itashimasɯ.

Dōryō: Kochira kara o-kake shimashō ka.

Deibiddo Sɯmisu: Ie, kore kara gaishutsu shimasɯ node, watashi kara o-denwa sashi-agemasɯ.

Dōryō: Wakarimashi̇ta. Sore de wa ...

Deibiddo Sɯmisu: De wa, shitsurei shimasɯ.

Switchboard: *Nanbu Department Store.*
David Smith: *Mr Suzuki in the 3rd sales section, please.*
Switchboard: *Please wait a moment.*
Colleague: *Hello. Can I help you? Unfortunately,*
Mr Suzuki has gone out.
David Smith: *What time is he coming back?*
Colleague: *He's due back at three.*
David Smith: *In that case, I'll phone again at three.*
Colleague: *Shall I get him to call you? (Literally, 'Shall he*
call you?')
David Smith: *No, I'm just about to go out, so I'll phone him.*
Colleague: *Fine, thank you. Goodbye.*
David Smith: *Goodbye.*

Notes on Conversation 12

a) In **Aite ga fuzai no bāi** (literally, 'occasion of other person absent'), **ga** indicates the subject of **fuzai** ('absent'). **Aite ga fuzai** ('other person's absence') describes **bāi** ('occasion') and so is linked to **bāi** with **no**.

b) **Shibaraku o-machi kudasai** is an Honorific form of **Chotto matte kudasai** ('Please wait a moment'). It is less polite than **Shōshō o-machi kudasai**.

c) **O-denwa kawarimashita** (literally, 'The phone has changed') is a set phrase used when a call has been transferred.

d) **3(San)-ji ni modoru yotei desu** means 'He is scheduled (to be back) at three o'clock'. **Yotei da** after the Plain present adds the meaning 'be scheduled to'.

e) **O-denwa sashi-ageru** ('make a phone call') is Hum. of **denwa o kakeru**. **Watashi kara** (literally, 'from me') is best translated as 'from here' in this case.
Note that there are two other less polite Humble expressions meaning 'to make a phone call' in the conversation: **o-kake suru** and **o-denwa itasu**.

f) **Shitsurei shimasu** ('Goodbye') means literally, 'I will be rude (and go).'

g) New words:

ainiku	unfortunately
aite	other person, partner
bāi	occasion; when
denwa suru =	
denwa o kakeru	phone
dōryō	colleague
fuzai	being out/absent
modorareru	return (Passive of **modoru** used as Hon.)
node = **kara**	so (see Structure 37)
shibaraku	a short while
yotei	schedule

INFORMATION: The Japanese transport system

Getting to Tokyo from Narita Airport

Certain hotels are served by an airport bus ('Limousine Bus'). If you are not sure whether your hotel is one of these, check with airport information, or, in advance, with JNTO. Limousine Buses run from outside the terminal building and are convenient if somewhat expensive. The bus may be rather slow in the rush-hour (from 7.00 to 9.00 in the morning and from 5.00 to 6.00 in the evening).

Alternatively, Keisei and JR run trains to central Tokyo. The JR trains (called 'N'EX' for 'Narita Express') are generally more expensive, but may be more convenient, as there are trains to Tōkyō, Ikebukuro, Shinjuku and Yokohama. Keisei express trains ('Skyliners') only run to Ueno, although slow trains run to stations on the Toei Asakusa line.

The hazards of taking taxis

Do not take a taxi from Narita to central Tokyo, unless you have money to burn. Because of traffic congestion, it is best to avoid taking taxis long distance in the Tokyo area. Moreover, because of the greater complexity of the Japanese address system (houses are numbered according to the order in which they were built on a particular plot of land, so number 1 could be between number 7 and number 43!), there is no guarantee that the driver will be able to find your destination address without some help, unless it is a well-known building. The fare could easily amount to several hundred pounds in the rush-hour.

The Tokyo transport system

Tokyo has 3 basic railway systems, JR, Eidan (Rapid Transit Authority) and Toei (Tokyo Municipal Authority). There are also private railways which terminate at Tokyo stations such as Shinjuku and Shibuya.

It is cheapest to use only one system for a trip, as every time you change system, you will have to pay a basic fare again. You may be able to buy a ticket for a through trip on two systems, changing at a certain station.

Station names are always labelled clearly in English on the platforms and on destination boards of trains. Many trains have electronic panels in the carriages giving information in English.

Buses are punctual, as their routes are usually short, serving to link stations.

Internal flights

Try to avoid having to transfer to Haneda Airport which is right on the other side of Tokyo. It is worth stressing Tokyo Narita when booking an internal flight. However, it is often more convenient to travel by train, particularly if your destination is served by the Bullet Train.

UNIT FIVE

Here we meet the first of two sorts of Japanese adjectives; the Plain negative forms of verbs; and how to say 'I want to ...' and 'probably'.

Structure 40: I adjectives

Kono konpyūtā wa <u>atarashii</u> desψ.
This computer is <u>new</u>.
Sono heya wa <u>hiroi</u> desψ ka. Hai, kanari <u>hiroi</u> desψ.
Is that room <u>big</u>? Yes, it is quite <u>big</u>.
Nihon-go wa <u>yasashii</u> desψ ka.
Is Japanese <u>easy</u>?

CHECKNOTES 40

a) There are two sorts of adjectives in Japanese: 'I adjectives' and 'Na adjectives' (see Unit Six). I adjectives are so called because their Plain present forms end in -ai, -ii, -ui or -oi. Adjectives ending in anything else (including -ei or consonant + i) are Na adjectives.

b) As with verbs, adjectives also have Plain and Polite forms. The Polite present of I adjectives is made from the Plain present by adding desψ. For example, shiroi (Plain present for 'is/are white') becomes shiroi desψ in the Polite present.

Checklist 40

aoi	blue
hazukashii	embarrassed
hidoi	awful
hiroi	wide; big (of rooms, etc.)
ii	good, nice
isogashii	busy; Hon. **o-isogashii**
kiiroi	yellow

kuroi	black
shiroi	white
tanoshii	enjoyable
ureshii	happy
yasashii	easy; nice (of people)
hana	flower
kanari	quite

FLUENCY PRACTICE 40
Translate the following sentences into English:

1 Kuroi desɰ.
2 Watashi wa ureshii desɰ.
3 Kono hana wa akai desɰ.
4 Hazukashii desɰ ka.
5 Sono hito wa hidoi desɰ.

Translate the following sentences into Japanese:

6 It is white.
7 These books are yellow.
8 Are those flowers blue?
9 It is very enjoyable.
10 Are [you] busy now? (Use **o-isogashii**.)

Structure 41: The position of adjectives

Kore wa <u>semai</u> heya desɰ.
This is a <u>small</u> room.
Sore wa <u>kuroi</u> jidō-sha desɰ ka. Iie, <u>shiroi</u> jidō-sha desɰ.
Is that a <u>black</u> car? No, it is a <u>white</u> car.
<u>Ii</u> o-tenki desu ne.
<u>Nice</u> weather, isn't it?

CHECKNOTES 41
a) Adjectives precede the nouns which they describe, as in English. For example, **ii o-tenki** ('<u>nice</u> weather').

Checklist 41

chiisai	small
furui	old
kibishii	strict
ōkii	big
semai	narrow, small (of room, etc.)
warui	bad ·
biru	building (short for **birudingu**)
hanashi	story (from **hanasu**, 'speak')
kangae	idea (from **kangaeru**, 'think')
o-tenki	Polite form of **tenki** weather
motto	more

FLUENCY PRACTICE 41
Translate the following sentences into English:

1 Ii kangae desψ.
2 Kanojo wa omoshiroi hito desψ.
3 Ōkii kaisha desψ ka. Iie, chiisai kaisha desψ.
4 Soko wa furui kaisha desψ.
5 Motto omoshiroi eiga wa arimasen ka.

Translate the following sentences into Japanese:

6 That is a new building.
7 Is that a red car?
8 That's a really interesting story.
9 He isn't a bad person.
10 She isn't a strict teacher.

Structure 42: Adverbs

Watashi-tachi wa <u>hayaku</u> okimashita.
We got up <u>early</u>.
<u>Samuku</u> narimashita.
It's got <u>cold</u>.
<u>Osoku</u> natte mōshiwake arimasen.
Sorry for being (literally, 'getting') <u>late</u>.

CHECKNOTES 42

a) Adverbs are formed from **I** adjectives by replacing the **-i** with **-ku**. We will call this the adverbial form.

b) Note that with **naru** ('become', 'get'), one needs to use an <u>adverb</u> in Japanese, for example: **atatakaku naru** ('get/become warm(er)'; literally, 'warmly').

c) Note that when an adjective ending in **-shii** is made into an adverb, it will then end in **-shiku**, with a silent 'i'.

Checklist 42

atatakai	warm
atsui	hot
hayai	quick; early
kurai	dark
osoi	late
samui	cold
yasui	cheap
yoku	well (irregular adverbial form of **ii**, 'good', 'fine')
fu-keiki	recession
mōshi-wake arimasen	I'm sorry (literally, 'there is/I have no excuse')
nedan	price
saikin	recently
shiru	know (Consonant verb). For example, **Shitte imasu** ('I, etc. know', literally, 'am knowing') but **Shirimasen** ('I, etc. don't know').

FLUENCY PRACTICE 42

Translate the following sentences into English:

1 Totemo atatakaku narimashita.
2 Hikō-ki wa osoku tsukimashita.
3 Sono kaisha no kabu wa saikin takaku narimashita.
4 Nihon-go wa yoku wakarimasu ga, hanasu koto wa dekimasen.
5 Sono shōhin no nedan wa fu-keiki de yasuku narimashita.

Translate the following sentences into Japanese:
6 We arrived late.
7 [It]'s gone dark.
8 [It]'s got very hot.
9 I know (literally, 'am knowing') that person well.
10 Mr Kaneko bought a watch cheaply.

Structure 43: The past of I adjectives

Samukatta des⍵ ka.
Was it cold?
Sore wa sugokatta/hidokatta des⍵.
That was amazing/awful.
Kinō wa atsukatta/atatakakatta/suzushɨkatta/samukatta des⍵.
It was hot/warm/cool/cold yesterday.

CHECKNOTES 43

a) The Plain past of I adjectives is formed by replacing the -i with
-katta. For example, takai ('high', 'expensive') becomes
takakatta ('was high/expensive').

The Polite past is formed by adding des⍵: -katta des⍵. The
correct Polite past for 'It was funny' is Okashɨkatta des⍵.
Even advanced learners of Japanese often translate from
English and produce incorrect forms like 'Okashii deshita'.
Such forms do NOT exist.

b) Note that the Plain past form of an adjective ending in -shii will
end in -shɨkatta with a devoiced 'i'.

c) Note that ii ('good', 'all right') has an irregular Plain past form:
yokatta. In fact, the stem of ii is yo- in all forms except ii itself
(which has a formal/old alternative, yoi).

Checklist 43

mushi-atsui	humid (from **musu**, 'steam', and **atsui**, 'hot')
okashii	funny
suzushii	cool
tadashii	correct
happyō	presentation
kinō	yesterday
natsu	summer
pātī	party

FLUENCY PRACTICE 43

Translate the following sentences into English:

1 Suzuki-san no happyō wa omoshirokatta desɰ ka.
2 Hakata Denki no kabu wa yasɰkatta desɰ.
3 Watashi wa isogashɨkatta desɰ.
4 Sono hoteru wa yokatta desɰ.
5 Pātī wa totemo tanoshɨkatta desɰ.

Translate the following sentences into Japanese:

6 I was embarrassed.
7 Yesterday was cool.
8 Was that translation expensive?
9 That product (over there) was very cheap.
10 The Japanese summer last year (**kyonen no Nihon no natsu**) was humid.

Structure 44: Negative I adjectives

Omoshiroi desɰ ka. Iie, <u>omoshiroku arimasen</u>.
Is it interesting? No, it <u>isn't interesting</u>.
Suzushii desɰ ka. Iie, zenzen <u>suzushɨku arimasen</u>.
Is it cool? No, it <u>isn't cool</u> at all.
Isogashii desɰ ka. Iie, amari <u>isogashɨku arimasen</u>.
Are you busy? No, <u>I'm not</u> very <u>busy</u>.
Tenki wa <u>yoku nai desɰ</u>.
The weather <u>is bad</u> (literally, 'not good').

CHECKNOTES 44

a) The Plain present negative of **l** adjectives is made by replacing **-i** with **-ku nai**. Adjectives ending in **-shii** have the form **-shiku nai** with a devoiced 'i'.

The Polite present negative is then formed by replacing **nai** with **arimasen**.

Alternatively, the Polite present negative may be formed by replacing **-i** with **-ku nai desu**. This latter form is considered substandard, but is common and sounds less abrupt than the form with **-ku arimasen**.

b) **Amari** ('very') and **zenzen** ('at all') are always used with a negative adjective or verb. Colloquially, **amari** is often pronounced '**anmari**'.

c) **Sonna ni** ('such a'; 'so') is usually used with a negative adjective or verb, for example: **Kare wa sonna ni kibishii sensei de wa arimasen** ('He isn't such a strict teacher').

Checklist 44

oishii	tasty, delicious
urayamashii	envious
bunpō	grammar
jōdan	joke
kanji	Chinese characters (as used in Japanese)
ryōri	cooking

FLUENCY PRACTICE 44

Translate the following sentences into English:

1 Urayamashii desu ka. Iie, urayamashiku arimasen.
2 Nihon-go no bunpō wa muzukashii desu ka. Iie, sonna ni muzukashiku arimasen.
3 Sono jōdan wa okashii desu ka. Iie, zenzen okashiku arimasen.
4 Kono ryōri wa amari oishiku arimasen.
5 Sono shōhin wa takaku arimasen.

Translate the following sentences into Japanese:

6   [It]'s not cheap.
7   Is [it] hot? No, [it] isn't hot. [It]'s cool.
8   Is [it] expensive? No, [it] isn't at all expensive.
9   Are kanji difficult? No, [they] aren't at all difficult.
10 Is that story interesting? No, [it]'s not very interesting.

Structure 45: Plain past negative I adjectives

Samukatta desɰ ka. Iie, zenzen samuku arimasen deshɨta.
Was it cold? No, it wasn't at all cold.
Ototoi no tenki wa dō deshɨta ka. Amari yoku arimasen
deshɨta.
How was the weather the day before yesterday? It wasn't very good.

CHECKNOTES 45

a) The Plain past negative of I adjectives is formed by putting the
nai of the -ku nai structure (Structure 44, note a) into the past
form: -ku nakatta.

The Polite past negative is then formed by replacing nakatta
with arimasen deshɨta.

It is also possible to form the Polite past negative by putting
-ku nai desɰ into the past: -ku nakatta desɰ. Beware!
Learners of Japanese often produce forms like 'atatakaku nai
deshɨta' instead of atatakaku arimasen deshɨta. This does
not work!

Checklist 45

dō   how (not as polite as ikaga)

FLUENCY PRACTICE 45

Translate the following sentences into English:

1 Amari muzukashɨku arimasen deshɨta.
2 Zenzen isogashɨku arimasen deshɨta.
3 Sono resɰtoran no ryōri wa amari oishɨku arimasen deshɨta.
4 Kinō pasokon o kaimashɨta ga, yasɰku arimasen deshɨta.
5 Suzuki-san no sɰpīchi wa amari omoshiroku arimasen deshɨta.

Translate the following sentences into Japanese:

6 The present wasn't so expensive.
7 The exam wasn't at all easy.
8 The conference wasn't very interesting.
9 The consultant's presentation wasn't at all interesting.
10 Was the party enjoyable? No, it wasn't at all enjoyable.

Structure 46: -te form of I adjectives

Kono shina-mono wa yasɰkte ii desɰ.
These goods are cheap and good.
Sono hon wa nagakɰte tsumaranai desɰ.
That book is long and boring.

CHECKNOTES 46

a) Like verbs (see Structure 31), adjectives also have **-te** forms. The basic meaning is 'and', although, especially with adjective **-te** forms, there is often the sense that the first clause caused the second.

b) The **-te** form of I adjectives is formed by adding **-te** to the adverbial form (which ends in **-ku**; see Structure 42): **-kɰte**. Note that the 'u' becomes silent in the process.

c) Like the **-te** form of verbs, the **-te** form of adjectives does not change for tense, so it may mean 'is', 'will be' or 'was (adj.) and ...'.

Checklist 46

yameru	give up
aburappoi	oily (from **abura**, 'oil', and **-ppoi**, '-ish')
katai	hard
kitanai	dirty
mazui	unpleasant (to eat)
nagai	long
suppai	sour
tsumaranai	boring
tsumetai	cold (drinks; people in their relations with others); **samui** is used for 'cold', of weather or people feeling physically cold
fuyu	winter
ringo	apple
shina-mono	goods (**mono** means 'thing')

FLUENCY PRACTICE 46
Translate the following sentences into English:

1 Ringo wa katakɯte suppakatta desɯ.
2 Muzukashɨkɯte yamemashɨta.
3 Isogashɨkɯte kaigi ni ikimasen deshɨta.
4 Kono apāto wa hirokɯte ii desu ne.
5 Atsɯkɯte benkyō dekimasen deshɨta. (**Suru koto ga** is omitted).

Translate the following sentences into Japanese:

6 This beer is deliciously cold (literally, 'cold and delicious').
7 The room was cramped and dirty.
8 The British winter is long and cold.
9 That shop's cooking is oily and unpleasant.
10 That café is expensive and [the food] isn't tasty.

Structure 47: Plain negative forms of verbs

<u>Ikanai?</u>
<u>Aren't</u> you <u>going</u>?
<u>Kaeranakatta.</u>
He, etc. <u>did not go home.</u>
<u>Nanimo shinakatta.</u>
He, etc. <u>did nothing.</u>
Basu ga <u>konak</u>ɯte komarimashɨta.
I was in a fix, <u>as</u> the bus <u>didn't come.</u>
Kore wa enpitsu <u>de wa nak</u>ɯte, bōrupen desɯ.
This <u>isn't</u> a pencil, <u>(and)</u> it's a ballpoint pen.

CHECKNOTES 47

a) Plain present negative and Plain past negative verb forms end in **-nai** and **-nakatta** respectively. You will notice that these forms look rather like **I** adjectives, and they do, in fact, behave like them in many respects. The stems to which these endings are added are as follows:

Consonant verbs replace **-u** with **-a̲.nai** and **-a̲.nakatta**. For example, **hanaS.u** → **hanaS.a̲.nai**.

Vowel verbs replace **-ru** with **-nai** and **-nakatta**. For example, **tabE.ru** → **tabE.nai**.

b) **Da** has the forms **de wa nai** and **de wa nakatta**. **Suru** has the forms **shɨ.nai** and **shɨ.nakatta**. **Kuru** has the forms **konai** and **konakatta**.

c) The negative **-te** form is made by replacing **-nai** with **-nak**ɯte. However, note that it cannot be used before **kudasai** (see Structure 55). It has the meaning 'it doesn't ..., (and) it ...'.

d) In colloquial speech, **des**ɯ is often attached to the **-nai** and **-nakatta** forms to make alternatives to **-masen** and **-masen deshɨta**. For example, **Ikanai des**ɯ **ka** is used instead of **Ikimasen ka** ('Aren't you going?').

Checklist 47

suru	do, make; ... **ni suru** make it ..., decide on ..., have ...
tomaru	stay (takes **ni**, not **de**, to indicate place)
boku	I (Plain form of **watashi**; used only by men)
bōrupen	ballpoint pen
ichi-man'en-satsu	¥10,000 note

FLUENCY PRACTICE 47

Translate the following sentences into English:

1 Wakaranai.
2 Issho ni ikanai?
3 Sore de wa nakψte, kore ni shimasψ.
4 Zenzen Nihon-go ga dekinai.
5 Jisho ga nakψte, komatta.

Translate the following sentences into Japanese, using Plain forms:

6 This isn't a ¥10,000 note.
7 Won't you have a drink?
8 Won't you watch Japanese television?
9 He's not an accountant, (and) [he]'s a lawyer.
10 I (masculine) didn't stay in a good hotel.

Structure 48: Wanting to do something

Ōsaka ni <u>ikitai desψ</u>.
I <u>want to go</u> to Osaka.
Takahashi-san ni <u>meiwaku o kaketaku arimasen deshita</u>.
I <u>didn't want to be a nuisance</u> to Mr Takahashi.
Kaigi <u>ni detaku arimasen deshita</u>.
I <u>didn't want to attend</u> the conference.

CHECKNOTES 48

a) The idea of 'wanting to do something' is expressed by removing **-masu** from the verb and adding **-tai desu** to the **masu** stem thus formed. For example, **Ōsaka ni ikimasu** ('I'm going to Osaka') becomes **Ōsaka ni ikitai desu** ('I want to go to Osaka').

b) Normally **-tai** is used only when the subject is 'I', so it is not necessary to use **watashi**, etc. When the subject is not 'I', (verb)-**tagaru** is sometimes used: **Uchi no shachō wa tasha to keiyaku o musubitagatte imasu** ('Our company president wants [literally, 'is wanting'] to enter into a contract with another company'). However, often it is best to avoid expressing such ideas, as it is felt to be presumptuous to draw attention to the desires of others!

c) **-tai** behaves as if it were an **I** adjective. So, the past and negative forms are:

Polite past: **Ikitakatta desu** ('I wanted to go')
Polite present negative: **Ikitaku arimasen** (or **Ikitaku nai desu**) ('I don't want to go')
Polite past negative: **Ikitaku arimasen deshita** (or **Ikitaku nakatta desu**) ('I didn't want to go')
-te form: **Ikitakute** ('I want[ed] to go and ...')
negative **-te** form: **Ikitaku nakute** ('I don't/didn't want to go and ...')

d) Traditionally, the object in sentences with **-tai** was indicated by **ga**. Nowadays, one hears both **o** and **ga**.

Checklist 48

aruite iku	walk ('to' = **made**, not **ni** as you might expect)
meiwaku	nuisance; **meiwaku o kakeru** be a nuisance (to somebody)
koto	thing (abstract)
ni tsuite	about (follows noun)
tasha	another company
tenji-kai	trade fair
uchi	inside; **uchi no** our (literally, 'of/belonging to inside')

FLUENCY PRACTICE 48
Translate the following sentences into English:

1 Ginza made aruite ikitai desu ne.
2 Ototoi Tōkyō no tenji-kai ni ikitakatta desu.
3 Nihon no omiyage o kaitakatta desu.
4 Kawaguchi-san ni meiwaku o kaketaku arimasen deshita.
5 Tanaka-san wa sono koto ni tsuite hanashitaku arimasen deshita.

Translate the following sentences into Japanese:

6 [I] want to eat sushi.
7 [I] want to send a fax to the U.K.
8 [I] want to see that film.
9 [I] want to go to Japan.
10 [I] want to study Japanese.

Structure 49: ... deshō ('probably')

(Tabun) ame ga furu deshō.
It will probably rain.
Komaru deshō.
That must be a nuisance (for you).
Kyō wa kinō yori atatakai deshō.
Today is probably warmer than yesterday.
Nihon-go wa muzukashii deshō.
Japanese must be difficult for you.

CHECKNOTES 49

a) Adding deshō (Polite form) or darō (Plain form) to Plain style verbs and adjectives expresses the idea of 'probably'. Da ('is', 'are', etc.) drops out before deshō and darō. Tabun ('probably') is often added, somewhat unnecessarily!

b) Deshō is also used as a polite alternative to desu: O-nomimono wa ikaga deshō ka ('Would you like something to drink?').

c) To say that something or somebody is 'more (adjective) than' another, use yori. Its position is after the second noun and before the adjective.

Checklist 49

ame	rain; **ame ga furu** to rain
mō	already; more
Roshia-go	Russian (language)
shisha	branch (of a company)
yuki	snow; **yuki ga furu** to snow

FLUENCY PRACTICE 49

Translate the following sentences into English:

1 Tabun Ōsaka no shisha ni wa ikanai deshō.
2 Shinbun kisha wa tabun kiji o kaite iru deshō.
3 Ocha wa ikaga deshō ka.
4 Tanaka-san wa mō Nihon ni tsuita deshō.
5 Roshia-go wa Eigo yori muzukashii deshō.

Translate the following sentences into Japanese:

6 [It] will probably snow tomorrow.
7 Japanese must be very difficult.
8 [You] probably don't want to meet Mr Kawasaki.
9 The hotel was probably expensive.
10 I've already posted the report, so it will probably be all right.
(Use **daijōbu da** for 'be all right' – see Unit Six – rather than
ii, which would sound negligent here!)

CONVERSATION 13: **O-tenki**
('The weather')

Contrary to popular belief, the British are not the only people who enjoy talking about the weather! It is also a popular 'safe subject' in Japan.

Yoshioka: Totemo samuku narimashita ne.
Deibiddo Sumisu: Ē, demo narete imasu kara ... Igirisu no fuyu mo konna kanji desu.

Yoshioka: *It has gone very cold, hasn't it?*
David Smith: *Yes, but I'm used to it. British winter is also like this.*

Notes on Conversation 13

a) **Ē, demo narete imasu kara** means literally 'Yes, but I'm used to (it), so ...'. The Japanese have a love of incomplete sentences, as they are vaguer and, therefore, more polite.

b) **Konna kanji desu** means literally 'is this sort of feeling'.

c) New words:
   nareru get used; **narete iru** be used ('to' is **ni**)

   demo but
   kanji feeling
   konna this sort of, such

CONVERSATION 14: **O-hisashi-buri desu ne!**
('I haven't seen you for ages!')

Deibiddo Sɯmisu: Yā, Itō-san! O-hisashi-buri desu ne! O-genki deshɨta ka.

Itō: Hai, o-kage-sama de totemo genki desɯ. Sɯmisu-san mo o-genki desɯ ka.

Deibiddo Sɯmisu: Hai, o-kage-sama de ... Senjitsu, Makuhari Messe no tenji-kai de Sɯmisu shōkai no Kaneko-san ni aimashɨta yo.

Itō: Sō desɯ ka. Kaneko-san mo o-isogashii yō desu ne.

Deibiddo Sɯmisu: Ē, tsugi no tenji-kai ni mo deru to itte imashɨta kara, Itō-san mo chikai uchi ni o-ai dekiru deshō.

David Smith: Oh, Mr Itoh! I haven't seen you for ages! How have you been?

Itoh: I've been fine, thanks. How are you?

David Smith: Fine, thanks. I met Mr Kaneko from Smith and Co. at an exhibition at Makuhari Messe the other day.

Itoh: Really? (Literally, 'Is it so?') Mr Kaneko seems to be busy too, doesn't he?

David Smith: Yes, he was saying that he'd go to the next exhibition too, so you'll probably be seeing him in the near future.

Notes on Conversation 14

a) **Yā** ('Oh!') is an exclamation used to attract somebody's attention.

b) **O-hisashi-buri desu ne** is a set phrase meaning 'It's been a long time since I've seen you.'

c) **Genki** means 'well', if you are talking about yourself. If referring to other people, remember to use the Honorific **o-genki**.

d) **O-kage-sama de** means literally 'thanks to you'. It can be used on its own in reply to **O-genki desɯ ka**, or together with a phrase like **genki desɯ**.

e) In ... **Kaneko-san ni aimashɨta yo** ('I met Mr Kaneko ...'), **yo** adds an assertive, friendly tone. It is best not to use it too much to superiors.

f) (Plain style adjective) **yō desɯ** means 'seems (adjective)'. **Yō desɯ** is used when one has evidence, usually visual, of something. (See Structure 73.)

g) ... **to itte imashɨta** is used for 'was saying that ...'. See Structure 60.

h) **O-ai dekiru** ('be able to meet') is the Honorific form of **au koto ga dekiru.**

i) New words:
   chikai uchi ni   soon, in the near future
   senjitsu   the other day (Polite form of **kono aida**)
   shōkai   and Co.

CONVERSATION 15: **Yakɯsoku no jikan henkō** ('Changing the time of one's appointment')

Deibiddo Sɯmisu: Moshimoshi, eigyō 3(san)-ka no Suzuki-san o o-negai shimasɯ.
Uketsuke no hɨto: Shōshō o-machi kudasai.
    Suzuki: Moshimoshi, Suzuki desu ga ...
Deibiddo Sɯmisu: Moshimoshi, Roiyaru Fānichā no Sɯmisu desɯ. 10(tō)ka no mītingu no ken desu ga, mōshiwake arimasen ga, jikan o 1(ichi)-jikan osoku shɨte itadakemasen deshō ka. Nagoya kara no Shinkansen ga konzatsu shɨte ite, osoi ressha no kippu shɨka torenakatta mono desɯ kara.
    Suzuki: Ii desɯ yo. De wa 2(ni)-ji ni henkō shimashō.
Deibiddo Sɯmisu: Dōmo arigatō gozaimasɯ.

David Smith: Hello, Mr Suzuki in the 3rd sales section, please.
Receptionist: Please wait a moment.
    Suzuki: Hello, Suzuki here.
David Smith: Hello, this is Smith from Royal Furniture. It's about the meeting on the 10th. I'm sorry, but could we make it about an hour later? The Bullet Trains from Nagoya are crowded, so I could only get a ticket for a later train.
    Suzuki: That's all right. Let's change it to two o'clock, then.
David Smith: Thank you.

Notes on Conversation 15

a) **Tōka** means 'the tenth'. The basic counter for days of the month is **-nichi**, but there are many irregular forms: **tsuitachi** the 1st (day of the month), **ichi-nichi** one day, **futsuka** 2nd or 2 days, **mikka** 3rd or 3 days, **yokka** 4th or 4 days, **itsuka** 5th or 5 days, **muika** 6th or 6 days, **nanoka** 7th or 7 days, **yōka** 8th or 8 days, **kokonoka** 9th or 9 days, **tōka** 10th or 10 days, **jū-ichi-nichi** 11th or 11 days. After this, forms are regular except for: **jū-yokka** 14th or 14 days, **jū-kunichi** 19th or 19 days, **hatsuka** 20th or 20 days, **ni-jū-yokka** 24th or 24 days and **ni-jū-kunichi** 29th or 29 days.

b) **Mītingu no ken desu ga ...** means 'It's about the meeting, but ...'. **Ken** literally means 'matter'.

c) **Jikan** means 'time'. It is also a counter for hours. Note **yojikan** ('4 hours').

d) In **jikan o** 1-**jikan osuku shite itadakemasen deshō ka**, ... **o osoku suru** means 'to make ... later'. (Verb)-**te itadakemasen ka** literally means 'Couldn't I receive (Hum.) your ...ing', 'Couldn't I get you to ...'.

e) **Nagoya kara no Shinkansen** means 'the Bullet Train from Nagoya'. **No** is required to make **Nagoya kara** describe **Shinkansen**.

f) **Shika** ('only') always goes with a negative verb or adjective. For example: **Tamago ga mittsu shika nai** ('There are only three eggs [tamago]').

g) **Mono desu kara** adds the implication 'and so naturally (I did what I did)'.

h) **Ii desu yo** ('That's all right') is said when somebody has apologized for something.

i) **Dōmo arigatō gozaimasu** ('thank you very much') is politer than **dōmo arigatō**.

j) New words:
henkō suru   change (arrangement, etc.); 'to' is **ni**
konzatsu suru   get crowded
  = **komu**
toru   take; (here) get; **toreru** is the Potential
                  (see Structure 69): 'be able to take/get'.
ressha   (long-distance) train (but **densha** is
                  'electric train', for commuting, etc.)

INFORMATION: Business meetings

Business card etiquette
When exchanging business cards, it is usual for the guest or, in situations where neither person is a guest, the younger person to offer his or her card first. Make sure that your card is the right way round, so that the other person can read it. Treat the other person's card with respect, putting it on the table in front of you if you are seated.

Bars
Don't be surprised if you get taken to several bars after you've been taken to dinner. This is known as **ni-ji-kai** (literally, 'second meeting'). Bars are often small rooms, so it is easy to relax and get to know people in an informal atmosphere. They often have facilities for **karaoke**. Turning down an invitation to go to another bar may be seen as an indication that you are not keen on getting to know the Japanese concerned better, or that you have little interest in the project you are discussing in 'work-time'.

In fact, the line between work and play in Japan often seems blurred to Westerners. This has the pleasant side-effect that Japanese people you worked closely with and whom you may have considered as work associates, may well be loyal, long-term friends!

One word of advice: **sake**, usually translated as 'rice wine', is best treated as a spirit!

How to say 'no' in Japan
It is important to avoid abrupt expressions meaning 'No' or 'I disagree'. If you do have to disagree, make it clear that you understand the merits of the other position and that your alteration

is only a minor one (however major it may be!) Expressions such as **Sō desu ne/nē** ('Is that so?'), **Naruhodo** ('Really?') or **Kangaete okimasⱳ** ('I'll think about it') often mean 'No'. Remember: being vague is, generally speaking, polite; being precise may be perceived as **rikutsuppoi** ('argumentative').

Thank you letter

After a visit to a Japanese organization, it is important to write a letter thanking those who showed you round. It does not need to be long and English will normally suffice. Not doing this is regarded as a major breach in etiquette, even if there is an awareness that such formalities are not treated so seriously in other countries.

It is usual to thank the people who looked after you during your visit, using such expressions as **Taihen o-sewa ni narimashіta** ('Thank you for everything you did for me'), when you next phone them, even if six months have elapsed since the visit.

Solving business problems

Because of cultural differences, including the Japanese use of vagueness as an indication of politeness, misunderstandings are common. This is often the stage when business arrangements fall through. Patience will be rewarded, but a few angry words could finish a long-term relationship.

The Japanese will never say 'No'! Don't think that you've got a 'yes' because they are smiling politely and saying **hai** or **ē** frequently. Most of the time these word means 'I am listening to you', rather than 'yes'. This also explains why **hai** and **ē** are used so frequently on the phone. A lack of such **aizuchi** ('interjections') when speaking Japanese will make the other person feel insecure.

The businesswoman in Japan

Although things are changing slowly, the world of business in Japan is still more male-dominated than in Britain. Women are often expected to stop working when they have children, and need to work harder to obtain managerial posts. Some Japanese men may feel disorientated or even threatened by a Western businesswoman.

UNIT SIX

Here we meet the other sort of Japanese adjective, the 'Na adjective', and learn how to say 'Is it all right to ...?', 'Please don't ...', and 'You mustn't ...'. Finally, the -n da construction is introduced.

Structure 50: Na adjectives

A', <u>taihen da</u>.
How <u>awful</u>! (Literally, 'Oh, it's awful!')
<u>Shizuka desu</u> ne.
<u>It's quiet</u>, isn't it?
<u>Daijōbu datta</u>.
<u>It was all right</u>.
Totemo <u>kantan deshita</u> ne.
It <u>was</u> very <u>simple</u>, wasn't it?
Sono repōto wa <u>yūmei de</u>, daredemo shitte imasʉ.
That report <u>is famous</u> and everybody knows (of) it.
Kare no jōdan wa <u>hontō ni</u> okashɨkatta desʉ.
His joke was <u>really</u> funny.

CHECKNOTES 50

a) As mentioned in Structure 40, '**Na** adjectives' are adjectives which end in anything except **-ai**, **-ii**, **-ui** or **-oi**.

b) The endings of **Na** adjectives are the same as for **da** ('is', 'are', etc.). Hence:

The Plain present of **Na** adjectives ends in **da**.
The Polite present is made by replacing **da** with **desʉ**.
The Plain past is made by replacing **da** with **datta**.
The Polite past is made by replacing **da** with **deshɨta**.
The **-te** form is made by replacing **da** with **de**.

c) In addition, it is possible to make adverbs by replacing **da** with **ni**. As with **I** adjectives, **naru** ('become', 'get') requires an adverb, for example: **kanō ni naru** ('become possible').

114

Checklist 50

shinrai suru	trust
a'	oh! (exclamation of surprise); often followed by a glottal stop, indicated here by a '
daredemo	everybody
benri da	convenient
byōki da	ill
fu-kanō da	impossible
genki da	well; lively
hitsuyō da	necessary
hontō da	true; **hontō ni** really
kanō da	possible
kantan da	simple
kokʉsai-teki da	international
shizuka da	quiet
shōjiki da	honest
taihen da	awful
urusai	noisy
yūmei da	famous

FLUENCY PRACTICE 50
Translate the following sentences into English:

1 O-genki desʉ ka. Hai, o kage-sama de.
2 Sumimasen ga, sore wa fu-kanō desʉ.
3 Sono hoteru wa shizuka desu ga, ano hoteru wa urusai desʉ.
4 Atarashii konpyūtā gā hitsuyō ni narimashɨta. (**Ga** rather than **wa** indicates the subject here, as new information is introduced.)
5 Nihon no chika-tetsu wa benri de yasui desʉ.

Translate the following sentences into Japanese:

6 My wife is ill.
7 I, etc. need this magazine. (This magazine is necessary.)
8 This product is very convenient.
9 He is an internationally famous architect.
10 He is honest and [you] can trust [him].

Structure 51: Adjectives before nouns

Hontō ni <u>suteki na</u> purezento desu.
It's a really <u>lovely</u> present.

CHECKNOTES 51

a) When a **Na** adjective comes before a noun, **da** is replaced by **na**.

b) Three **I** adjectives, **okii** ('big'), **chisaii** ('small') and **okashii** ('funny'), may be used as they are before a noun, but often the forms **ōki na**, **chiisa na** and **okashi na** are found. For example:

Okashi na hanashi desu ne. ('It's a funny story, [isn't it?]')
Okashii hanashi desu ne is also possible.

Forms such as 'ōki da', 'ōki datta', 'ōki de wa nai', etc., do NOT occur. Use **ōkii**, **ōkikatta**, **ōkiku nai**, etc., for 'big', 'was big', 'is not big', respectively.

c) There is a small group of adjectives, including **byōki da** ('ill'), **hontō da** ('true') and **tsugi da** ('next'), which take **no** instead of **na** when they come before a noun. They are best thought of as honorary **Na** adjectives, as all other forms are the same as for **Na** adjectives. From now on, they will be marked in the Checklists **byōki (no)**, etc.

Checklist 51

wasureru	forget
baka da	stupid
daiji da	important
iya da	unpleasant; dislike (see Structure 53)
kirei da	beautiful
nigiyaka da	lively
suteki da	lovely
joyū	actress (**haiyu** = actor)
keiken	experience
machi	street; town, city
niwa	garden

FLUENCY PRACTICE 51

Translate the following sentences into English:

1 Asoko wa kirei na niwa desu ne.
2 Amari kirei na biru de wa arimasen.
3 Rondon wa shizuka na machi de wa arimasen.
4 Baka na koto o shimashita.
5 Daiji na mono o wasuremashita.

Translate the following sentences into Japanese:

6 That is a big company.
7 This is a very convenient product.
8 That was an unpleasant experience.
9 Shibuya is a lively place (**machi**).
10 Mr Suzuki's wife is a famous actress.

Structure 52: Negative Na adjectives

Kyō amari <u>genki de wa nai</u>.
I, etc. <u>am not</u> very <u>well</u> today.
Koko wa zenzen <u>shizuka de wa arimasen</u>.
<u>It's not</u> at all <u>quiet</u> here.
Omotta hodo <u>fukuzatsu de wa nakatta</u>.
It wasn't as <u>complicated</u> as I, etc. had thought.
Nihon ryokō no shashin wa <u>kirei de wa arimasen deshita</u>.
The photographs from the Japan trip <u>were not beautiful</u>.
Kare wa amari <u>majime de wa nakute</u>, ichi-nichi-jū asonde iru yo.
He'<u>s not</u> very <u>serious</u> and plays (around) all day long.

CHECKNOTES 52

a) The Plain present negative is made by replacing **da** with **de wa nai**.

b) The Polite present negative is made by replacing **da** with **de wa arimasen**. (In colloquial speech, the Polite present negative may also be formed by replacing **da** with **de wa nai desu**.)

c) The Plain past negative is formed by replacing **da** with **de wa nakatta**.

d) The Polite past negative is formed by replacing **da** with **de wa arimasen deshita**. (Again, in colloquial speech, the Polite past negative may also be formed by replacing **da** with **de wa nakatta desu̶**.)

e) The negative **-te** form is made by replacing **da** with **de wa nak̶ute**.

Checklist 52

asobu	play
ichi-nichi-jū	all day long
omotta hodo	(set phrase) as I, etc. had thought
jōzu da	good at
majime da	serious (more positive in Japanese than in English)
omotta hodo	(set phrase) as I, etc. had thought
seikaku da	accurate
taisetsu da	important
tekitō da	suitable
basho	place; (here) location
kōen	park
ryokō	trip
sūji	figure

FLUENCY PRACTICE 52
Translate the following sentences into English:

1 Hitsuyō de wa arimasen deshita.
2 Kono sūji wa seikaku de wa arimasen.
3 Sono konsarutanto wa amari yūmei de wa arimasen.
4 Nihon-go wa su̶koshi dekimasu ga, jōzu de wa arimasen.
5 Nagoya no hoteru no basho wa amari benri de wa arimasen deshita.

Translate the following sentences into Japanese:

6 That isn't suitable.
7 The exam wasn't very simple.
8 The manual isn't complicated.
9 The park wasn't very quiet.
10 That wasn't very important.

Structure 53: Japanese adjectives → English verbs

> **Nihon ryōri ga suki desu.**
> I, etc. like Japanese cookery.
> **Nihon-go ga o-jōzu desu ne.**
> You are good at Japanese (aren't you)?

CHECKNOTES 53

a) Certain adjectives (both **I** adjectives like **hoshii** ['want'] and **Na** adjectives like **suki da** ['like'] and **kirai da** ['dislike']) translate into English as verbs.

b) Note that in such expressions, the objects take **ga** rather than **o**. (**Ga** normally indicates the subject.) For example, **Nomi-mono ga hoshii desu ne** ('I want a drink'). **Ne** is used here to soften the tone of the sentence, by seeking the agreement of the listener. Otherwise **hoshii desu** would sound rather abrupt.

c) **O-** may be used with **jōzu da** and **suki da**, when referring to other people 'being good at' and 'liking' things, respectively, in the same way as it is used with **O-genki desu ka** ('Are you well?').

Checklist 53

amai	sweet
heta da	be bad at
hoshii	want
itai	painful
kirai da	dislike
nigate da	be weak at
ōi	many
suki da	like
atama	head
firumu	film (for a camera)
ha	tooth
jogingu	jogging
nattō	fermented soya beans

musume	(my, etc.) daughter; **mus␙ko** my, etc. son
o-kashi	Japanese sweets/cakes
onaka	stomach
suiei	swimming
yaki-tori	Japanese-style grilled chicken

FLUENCY PRACTICE 53
Translate the following sentences into English:

1 Watashi wa Nihon-go ga nigate de ...
2 Yaki-tori wa o-s␙ki des␙ ka.
3 Kare wa suiei ga s␙ki de, watashi wa jogingu ga s␙ki des␙.
4 Kare-ra wa Nihon-go ga jōzu desu ga, watashi wa heta des␙.
5 Tōkyō wa hito ga ōi des␙.

Translate the following sentences into Japanese:

6 Do you like Japanese cakes?
7 [I] don't want that.
8 [I] have a head-ache/tooth-ache/stomach-ache.
9 [I]'m not good at Japanese.
10 My daughter dislikes nattō.

Structure 54: (Verb)-te mo ii des␙ ka ('May I ...')

> **Haitte mo ii des␙ ka.**
> Is it all right to go in?

CHECKNOTES 54
a) (Verb)-**te mo ii des␙ ka** is often translated as 'Is it all right to ...'
but the general sense it conveys equates to 'May I, etc. ...?',
'Is it O.K. if I, etc. ...?'

Checklist 54

akeru	open (something); but **aku** (something) opens
o-ai suru	meet (Hum.) ⎫
o-hanashi suru	speak (Hum.) ⎬ (See Structure 28, note a)
	⎭
mado	window

120

... ni tsuite	about ...;	**... ni tsuite hanasu** talk about ...;
yushutsu kachō	export director (literally, 'export section head')	

FLUENCY PRACTICE 54

Translate the following sentences into English:

1 Yushutsu kachō to o-hanashi shite mo ii deshō ka.
2 Shachō ni o-ai shite mo ii deshō ka.
3 Kaigi ni tsuite hanashite mo ii desu ka.
4 Denwa o shite/kakete mo ii desu ka.
5 Sukoshi koko de yasunde mo ii deshō ka.

Translate the following sentences into Japanese:

6 May [I] take photos?
7 Do you mind if [I] smoke?
8 Is [it] all right to read that newspaper?
9 Do you mind if [I] open a window?
10 Is [it] all right to speak in English?

Structure 55: (Verb)-naide kudasai ('Please don't ...')

Sono dentō o tsuke<u>naide kudasai</u>.
<u>Please don't</u> switch that light on.

CHECKNOTES 55

a) (Verb)-**naide kudasai** is the negative of (Verb)-**te kudasai** ('Please [verb]') (Structure 34). It is formed by attaching -**de kudasai** to the Plain present negative (Structure 44).

b) As we saw in Structure 36, **mae ni** means 'before ...ing' when used after the Plain present form of the verb: for example, **iku mae ni** ('before going'). When expressing the idea of before a point in time, **no mae ni** is normally used: for example, **moku-yōbi no mae ni** ('before Thursday'). However, **no** is dropped after -**ji** ('o'clock'): **ni-ji-mae ni** ('before two o'clock').

Checklist 55

enryo suru	be restrained (a virtue, in Japanese society), hold back
haku	wear (of trousers, footwear)
kiru	wear (of clothes); hence **ki-mono** literally, 'wear thing'
tsukeru	switch/turn/put on
dentō	(electric) light
ie	house
koe	voice; **ōki na koe de** in a loud (literally, 'big') voice
kutsu	shoes
naka	inside

FLUENCY PRACTICE 55

Translate the following sentences into English:

1 Tabako o suwanaide kudasai.
2 Koko de shashin o toranaide kudasai.
3 Enryo shinaide kudasai.
4 Raishū no happyō no mae ni nanimo iwanaide kudasai.
5 Roku-ji-mae ni denwa o kakenaide kudasai.

Translate the following sentences into Japanese:

6 Please don't use this [one].
7 Please don't push that button.
8 Please don't wear [your] shoes in the house (use **ie no naka de**).
9 Please don't go by taxi.
10 Please don't talk in a loud voice.

Structure 56: (verb)-te wa ikemasen ('mustn't')

Tabako o <u>sutte wa ikemasen</u>.
You/One <u>mustn't smoke</u>.

CHECKNOTES 56

a) The (verb)-**te wa ikemasen** structure is used most often when explaining signs and rules, rather than when telling other people what not to do!

Checklist 56

kamu	bite; but NOT in **hana o kamu** blow one's nose!
shigoto o suru	work
tomeru	stop (something) (takes **ni**, not **de**, to indicate place)
biza	viza
hakubutsu-kan	museum
hana	nose
hoka (no)	other
kōkyō (no)	public
meue no hito	a superior (literally, 'above', **ue**, 'the eyes', **me**)
-nashi ni	without ...
... no toki ni	during; **kaigi no toki ni** during the conference
yori saki ni	(do something) before (somebody) (follows noun)

FLUENCY PRACTICE 56

Translate the following sentences into English:

1 Hoka no kaisha no hito ni itte wa ikemasen.
2 Meue no hito yori saki ni kaette wa ikemasen.
3 Biza-nashi ni Nihon de shigoto o shite wa ikemasen.
4 Kōkyō no basho de hana o kande wa ikemasen.
5 Tosho-kan desu kara, ōki na koe de hanashite wa ikemasen.

Translate the following sentences into Japanese:

6 [You] mustn't take photos in the museum. (Use **hakubutsu-kan no naka de wa** – literally, 'at the museum's inside'.)
7 [You] mustn't stop [your] car there. (Use **ni**, not **de**, before **tomeru**.)
8 [You] mustn't wait there. (Use **matte iru** rather than **matsu**.)
9 [You] mustn't drink coffee before going to bed.
10 [You] mustn't speak English during the meeting.

Structure 57: (Plain verb/adjective) + n da

Jikan ga aru n desɯ ka.
So you've got time (on your hands), have you?
Dō shita n desɯ ka. Iya, daijōbu desɯ.
What's wrong? (Literally, 'How did you do?') I'm all right.

CHECKNOTES 57

a) **N da** has no direct equivalent in English. It is used extremely frequently to indicate that one is giving or requesting an explanation.

For example, if you had no evidence for it, but wanted to ask somebody if he or she was going out at some point, you would say: **Dekakemasɯ ka**.

If, however, you noticed that somebody was putting on his or her shoes, you could say **Dekakeru n desɯ ka**. In this situation, the Japanese can be paraphrased as something like 'So, you're going out, are you?'

b) When used in requests for help, **n desu ga ...** enables you to be vague (good in a Japanese context!) about the exact form of help you require:

Shinjuku ni ikitai n desu ga ... ('I'd like to go to Shinjuku, but ...').

c) The **n da** structure can cause offence (see the first example!), if wrongly used, so it is best not to use it unless you're sure it means what you want it to.

Checklist 57

hiku	catch (of colds)
tsuzukeru	continue (something); c.f. **tsuzuku** (something) continues
dono kurai	how long?
gurai	about (follows noun)
iya	no (not translatable here. Women would be more likely to use **ie** in this sort of context.)

-kagetsu	counter for months (duration). Note: 1 month: **ikkagetsu**; 6 months: **rokkaketsu**; 8 months: **hakkagetsu**; 10 months: **jukkagetsu (jikkagetsu)**
kaze	a cold; **kaze o hiku** catch a cold
kuwashii	detailed **kuwashɨku** in detail
-nen(kan)	counter for years (duration). Note: 4 years: **yonen(kan)**
tsukai-kata	how to use (from **tsukau**, 'use', and **kata**, 'way')

FLUENCY PRACTICE 57

Translate the following sentences into English:

1 Itta n desɰ ka.
2 Wāpɰro o kaitai n desu ga ...
3 Ōsaka Kagaku ni tsuite kuwashɨku shiritai n desu ga ...
4 Konpyūtā no tsukai-kata ga wakaranai n desu ga ...
5 Nihon-go ga jōzu desu ne. Dono kurai benkyō shita n desɰ ka. Yon-kagetsu gurai benkyō shimashɨta.

Translate the following sentences into Japanese:

6 [You]'re going home then?
7 I'd like to reserve a room.
8 I'd like to meet Miss Kurita.
9 What's wrong? [I]'ve got a head-ache.
10 [You]'re good at golf. How long have you been playing (Honorific)? [I]'ve been playing (Humble) for about four years. (Note that Japanese uses the present continuous [**-te iru**, etc.] when referring to actions which started in the past and continue into the present. English uses 'have been ...ing'.)

CONVERSATION 16: **Nihon-go ga o-jōzu desu ne**
('You're good at Japanese')

Mise no hito: Nihon-go ga o-jōzu desu ne.
Deibiddo Sumisu: Iya, sonna koto wa arimasen. Madamada
desu ...

Person in shop: You're good at Japanese.
David Smith: No, really. I'm still learning ...

Notes on Conversation 16

a) **Sonna koto wa arimasen** means literally 'there isn't such a thing'.

b) In **Madamada desu** ('I'm not [good at it] yet'), **madamada** means 'still', 'yet', and **desu** is being used to replace some expression meaning that one is not good at Japanese, in order to avoid accepting the compliment.

CONVERSATION 17: **Kaisha uketsuke nite**
('At the company reception')

Deibiddo Sumisu: Roiyaru Fānichā no Sumisu desu. Eigyō-bu
3(san)-ka no Suzuki-san ni o-ai shitai n desu ga.
Uketsuke no hito: Nan-ji no o-yakusoku desu ka.
Deibiddo Sumisu: 10(Jū)-ji desu.
Uketsuke no hito: Shōshō o-machi kudasai. Sore de wa, go-
annai itashimasu. (They walk down the
corridor.) Kochira e dōzo. Suzuki wa sugu ni
mairimasu node, o-kake ni natte o-machi
kudasai.
Deibiddo Sumisu: Hai, dōmo arigatō gozaimasu.

David Smith: I'm Smith from Royal Furniture. I'd like to see
Mr Suzuki in the 3rd sales section.
Receptionist: What time is your appointment?
David Smith: Ten o'clock.
Receptionist: Please wait a moment. I'll take you there ...
Please step this way. Mr Suzuki is on his way,
so please take a seat and wait (here).
David Smith: Thank you.

Notes on Conversation 17

a) **Go-annai itashimasѱ** ('I'll take you there') is the Humble form of **go-annai shimasѱ**, which, in turn, is the Humble form of **annai shimasѱ**. **Annai suru** means 'guide'.

b) New words and phrases:

Kochira e dōzo.	This way, please.
o-kake ni naru	Honorific form of **(koshi o) kakeru** sit
o-yakѱsoku	Honorific form of **yakѱsoku** appointment
sugu nl	immediately (**ni** makes **sugu** sound more precise)

CONVERSATION 18: Hoteru no resepѱshon nite: chekku auto
('At the hotel reception: checking out')

Deibiddo Sѱmisu: 1012 (Ichi zero ichi ni)-gōshitsu no Deibiddo Sѱmisu desѱ. Chekku auto o shitai n desu ga.

Uketsuke no hɨto: Shōshō o-machi kudasai. ... O-matase itashimashɨta. O-tomari to, go-riyō ni nararemashɨta o-denwa, o-shokuji, o-nomi-mono o fukumemashɨte ¥125,000 (jū-ni-man-go-sen'en) de gozaimasѱ. O-shiharai wa ikaga nasaimasѱ ka.

Deibiddo Sѱmisu: Kādo de o-negai shimasѱ.

Uketsuke no hɨto: Shōchi itashimashɨta. Kochira ni sain o o-negai shimasѱ.

Deibiddo Sѱmisu: Hai.

Uketsuke no hɨto: Arigatō gozaimashɨta. Kochira ga reshīto de gozaimasѱ.

David Smith: I'm David Smith from room 1012. I'd like to check out, please.

Receptionist: Please wait a moment. ... Sorry to keep you waiting. It's ¥125,000 including accommodation, telephone, food and drink. How would you like to pay?

David Smith: By card, please.

Receptionist: Thank you. Please sign here.

David Smith: Yes.

Receptionist: Thank you very much. This is your receipt.

Notes on Conversation 18

a) **O-matase itashimashita** ('Sorry to keep you waiting') is the Humble form of **O-matase shimashita**.

b) In **go-riyō ni nararemashita o-denwa** ('the telephone which you have used'), **go-riyō ni naru** is the Honorific form of **riyō suru** ('use'), which is more formal than **tsukau**. **Narareru** is the Passive of **naru**, here used as another Honorific expression. Putting the verb before **o-denwa** creates a relative clause, 'the telephone which you have used' (see Structure 61).

c) **... o fukumemashite** is the Polite form of **... o fukumete** ('including'). It is not usually necessary to use the form in **-mashite**, the Polite **-te** form, except in extremely polite speech.

d) **O-shiharai wa ikaga nasaimasu ka** ('How will you pay?') is literally 'What will you do (Honorific) about payment?'

e) **Kādo de o-negai shimasu** means '[I'd like to pay] by card please.'

f) **Shōchi itashimashita** is the Humble form of **Shōchi shimashita** ('certainly'). **Shōchi suru** literally means 'know', 'understand'. It is more formal than **wakaru**.

g) **Arigatō gozaimashita** ('thank you') is more polite than **arigatō gozaimasu**, but can only be used at the end of a conversation.

h) In **Kochira ga reshīto de gozaimasu**, **ga** is used instead of **wa**, as there has been no previous mention of the receipt.

i) New words:

kādo	(credit) card
o-shiharai	Hon. form of **shiharai** payment (from **harau**, 'pay')
o-shokuji	Hon. form of **shokuji** meal
o-tomari	Hon. form of **tomari** accommodation (from **tomaru**, 'stay'; 'stop')
reshīto = ryōshū-sho	receipt
sain	signature (from 'sign')

USEFUL PHRASES

Saying 'goodbye'
One of the most common ways for adults to say 'goodbye' is:
De wa, kore de shitsurei shimasu.
Shitsurei shimasu literally means 'to be rude', i.e. 'I'll be rude
(and go)'. **Kore de** means literally 'with this', but is untranslatable
here.

Sayōnara for 'goodbye' can sound a little childish. Beware:
English speakers tend to mispronounce it 'Sayonāra'.

Other useful phrases for when you leave
Sorosoro ... It's time I/we ... (literally, 'slowly'!)
De wa, raishū made. See you next week.
Chikai uchi ni mata o-ai shimashō. Let's meet again soon.

Thanking somebody for their help/time
Go-shinsetsu ni dōmo arigatō gozaimashita.
That's been very kind of you.

Here, **go-shinsetsu** is the Honorific form of **shinsetsu** ('kind').

O-sewa ni narimashita.
Thank you for being so helpful to me.

At the end of a meeting or tour
O-ai dekite totemo ureshii desu.
I'm very pleased to have met you.

O-ai dekiru is 'be able to meet' (Hum.). **Suru koto ga** is omitted.

(Kore kara mo) dōzo yoroshiku o-negai shimasu/itashimasu.
I look forward to your help/working with you (in the future).

INFORMATION: Etiquette

Politeness
Harmony and agreement are greatly valued in Japan, and it is considered impolite to be assertive about one's opinions, particularly where these differ from the general consensus. Clearly there will be certain situations where it is necessary to state one's opinion, for example when discussing a joint business plan, but it is advisable to emphasize the points of agreement before noting any possible bones of contention.

Punctuality
In Japan, it is usual to arrive 5 or 10 minutes early for a business appointment, and on time or 5 minutes late for a social appointment.

Bowing (ojigi)
The Japanese do not usually shake hands among themselves, as there is a taboo on physical contact in public. However, bowing is very common. People bow when they meet or part, and when they give each other things (such as presents and business cards). They also bow on the phone! Generally, the deeper the bow, the more politely it is perceived. You will find that you acquire this custom naturally. The main thing is to avoid exaggerated and jerky bowing.

Doing your groundwork (ne-mawashi)
Originally an agricultural term (literally, 'turning the roots') **ne-mawashi** (doing the groundwork) is how the Japanese avoid the damaging confrontations which afflict business in other countries. It involves checking that all parties are in agreement before decisions are made.

Debts of gratitude (on)
Most people who have been to Japan are struck with the generosity of the Japanese, and you are likely to return home laden with gifts.

However, a word of warning: each time you receive a present or favour, you incur **on** ('a debt of gratitude'). At some time in the future, you will need to pay back this **on**. This process is known as **on-gaeshi** (literally, 'returning the debt of gratitude'). If a gift strikes you as too extravagant, give some thought as to what may be expected in return.

Food
Most Japanese restaurants have plastic models of the food on the menu outside, which can always be used as a last resort if you are unlucky enough to find a restaurant without an English menu. Japanese food causes few problems, although it is probably a good idea to make up your mind whether you are going to be a **sushi-tsū** ('raw fish aficionado') in a Japanese restaurant in the U.K., before you go. The other main items which tend to cause problems are **nattō** ('fermented soya beans'), raw eggs (**nama-tamago**) and Japanese pickles (**tsuke-mono**).

Shoes
An invitation to visit a Japanese home is unusual and quite an honour. Should you be fortunate enough to receive one, it is important to remember that shoes are not generally worn in the home. These should therefore be removed in the hall.

Nose blowing
Never blow your nose in public in Japan. Nose blowing is perceived as a private activity, virtually in the same category as going to the toilet. Should the need arise, either excuse yourself and leave the room, or if necessary, try to survive with discreet suffering.

UNIT SEVEN

We will learn how to talk about past experiences, meet the Plain equivalent of -mashō ('let's') and see how to say 'say that ...' and 'think that ...'. This Unit also covers relative clauses in Japanese, verbs of giving and receiving, and how to say 'It's best to ...' and 'may'.

Structure 58: (verb)-ta koto ga aru

Nihon ni <u>itta koto ga arimasu</u>.
<u>I, etc. have been</u> to Japan.
Igirisu ni <u>itta koto ga arimasu ka</u>.
<u>Have you ever been</u> to the U.K.?

CHECKNOTES 58
a) (Verb)-**ta koto ga aru** indicates that one has had an experience. In questions, it corresponds to 'ever' in English.

Checklist 58

keiken suru	experience
Fuji-san	Mount Fuji
gaikoku	abroad
jishin	earthquake
Nihon-shu = Nihon no sake	Japanese rice wine

FLUENCY PRACTICE 58
Translate the following sentences into English:

1 Fuji-san o mita koto ga arimasu.
2 Nihon-shu o nonda koto ga arimasu.
3 Sono hon o yonda koto ga arimasu ka.
4 Gaikoku ni itta koto ga arimasu ka.
5 Jishin o keiken shita koto ga arimasu ka.

Translate the following sentences into Japanese:

6   I have made a speech at a conference.
7   Have you ever seen that film?
8   Have you ever been (gone) to Kyōto?
9   Did you ever study Japanese in Germany?
10   Have you ever eaten sushi?

Structure 59: (verb)-ō ('let's')

> **Ikō.**
> Let's go.
> **Ganbarō.**
> Let's do our best.

CHECKNOTES 59

a) (Verb)-**ō** is the Plain style equivalent of (verb)-**mashō** (see Structure 17). (Verb)-**ō ka** means 'shall we (verb)?'

b) The -**ō** form is made by replacing the final -**u** of the Plain present of a Consonant verb with -**ō**, and the final -**ru** of the Plain present of a Vowel verb with -**yō**. For example: **hanaS.u** → **hanaS.ō**; **tabE.ru** → **tabE.yō**.

c) **Da** has no -**ō** form, although one could use **ni narō**, from **ni naru** ('become'), in some situations. **Kuru** has **koyō** and **suru** has **shi.yō**.

Checklist 59

akirameru	give up
kiku	ask (somebody **ni**; something **o**)
gohan	meal (literally, 'rice')
onna no hito	woman

FLUENCY PRACTICE 59

Translate the following sentences into English:

1 Hajimeyō.
2 Hayaku neyō.
3 Ja, sugu ikō ka.
4 Asoko ni haitte, gohan o tabeyō.
5 Sono onna no hito ni kiite miyō (**kiite miru**, 'try asking').

Translate the following sentences into Japanese:

6 Let's finish. (Use **owari ni suru**.)
7 Shall we give up?
8 Let's go home. (Use **sorosoro**.)
9 Let's have a drink.
10 Let's check that at the hotel reception.

Structure 60: to yuu, to omou ('say that', 'think that')

Kare wa 'Ganbatte kudasai' to iimashita.
He <u>said</u>, 'Please do your best.'
Dame da to omoimasu.
I, etc. <u>think that</u> it's no good.
Ii to omoimasu yo.
I <u>think</u> it's all right.

CHECKNOTES 60

a) 'Say that ...' and 'think that ...' are expressed by using a sentence ending in the Plain style followed by ... **to yuu** ('say that ...') or ... **to omou** ('think that ...'). Polite style verbs may also be used if the original wording is being quoted.

b) In Japanese, the tense of the action of the verb before **to yuu** or **to omou** must be the same as that originally used by the person doing the saying or thinking.

c) If the subject of the verb before **to yuu** or **to omou** is mentioned, it is marked by **ga**, not **wa**.

Checklist 60

omou	think
dame da	no good

kenkyū kaihatsu	R & D (from **kenkyū**, 'research', and **kaihatsu**, 'development')
seiji	politics

FLUENCY PRACTICE 60
Translate the following sentences into English:

1 Kare wa kuru to iimashita.
2 Nihon ni ikitai to omoimasѱ.
3 Sono kata ga shachō da to omoimasѱ.
4 Watashi wa seiji ga omoshiroi to omoimasѱ.
5 Kenkyū kaihatsu ga taisetsu da to omoimasѱ ka.

Translate the following sentences into Japanese:

6 I think that hotel is all right.
7 I think that restaurant is expensive.
8 Mr Suzuki says that that hotel isn't good.
9 I thought that there were many problems.
10 He said that Japanese was very difficult.

Structure 61: Relative clauses

Watashi ga sengetsu katta hon wa omoshiroi desѱ.
The book which I bought last month is interesting.

CHECKNOTES 61

a) The Japanese for a relative clause like 'who are working in the U.K.' is **Igirisu de hataraite iru**; in other words, 'are working in the U.K.' in the Plain style. It is placed immediately before the noun it is describing, for example **Nihon-jin** ('Japanese people'), to produce **Igirisu de hataraite iru Nihon-jin** ('Japanese people who are working in the U.K.'). Note that there are no Japanese equivalents for relative pronouns such as 'that', 'which', 'who', 'where', 'when', etc.

b) The verbs and adjectives in Japanese relative clauses are usually in the Plain style, although the Polite style is possible in very polite speech.

c) If a subject occurs in a relative clause, it is marked by **ga**, not **wa**.

Checklist 61

de-au	meet unintentionally, bump into (object indicated by **ni**, not **o**)
happyō o suru	make a presentation
kenkyū suru	research
shōkai suru	introduce
tatsu	stand
... hodo (adjective)	as (adjective) as ...
josei no kata	Hon. of **onna no hito** woman
kankyō mondai	environmental problem (from **kankyō**, 'environment', and **mondai**, 'problem')
keizai-gaku	economics (from **keizai**, 'economy', and **-gaku**, 'study')
kikai	chance
otoko no hito	man
sengetsu	last month
sukunai	few

FLUENCY PRACTICE 61

Translate the following sentences into English. The nouns being described are underlined.

1 Happyō o shita <u>hito</u> wa donata desu ka.
2 Nihon-go o hanasu <u>kikai</u> wa sukunai desu. (Note: **wa** is needed here, not **ga**, as there is an idea of contrast – with one's opportunity to read Japanese, etc.)
3 Denwa de o-hanashi shita <u>ken</u> desu ga ...
4 Kore hodo furui kikai o tsukatte iru <u>kaisha</u> wa arimasen.
5 Pātī de wa Nihon no keizai-gaku o kenkyū shite iru <u>sensei</u> ni de-aimashita.

Translate the following sentences into Japanese:

6 I've sent the letter [I] wrote yesterday.
7 Who is the man who is standing over there?
8 Who was the woman (use **josei no kata**) whom Mr Nakamura introduced?
9 The conference I attended the day before yesterday wasn't very interesting.
10 The matter they talked [about] at the conference was the environmental problem.

Structure 62: Verbs of giving and receiving

Konsarutanto wa kono shorui o <u>kuremashita</u>.
The consultant <u>gave</u> me this document.
Tomodachi ni o-kashi o <u>agemashita</u>.
I <u>gave</u> my friend some Japanese cakes.
Buchō kara shiryō o <u>moraimashita</u>.
I <u>received</u> some materials/information from the department head.
Inu ni esa o <u>yarimashita</u>.
I <u>gave</u> some food to the dog.

CHECKNOTES 62

a) **Kureru** ('give') is used when somebody gives something to
   you or to somebody in your social group (for example, your
   family or company).

b) If you or somebody in your social group gives something to
   somebody, **ageru** is used (unless it is somebody of a lower
   status, or a plant or animal; then **yaru** is used). The person
   you give something to is indicated by **ni** ('to').

c) **Morau** is used when somebody in your group receives
   something. The person you receive something from is
   indicated by **kara** or **ni** ('from').

d) The Honorific form of **kureru** – **kudasaru** – and the Humble
   form of **morau** – **itadaku** – are in common use, even when
   respect language is not otherwise being used very much.

Checklist 62

itadaku	Hum. of **morau** receive
kudasaru	Hon. of **kureru** give (irreg. Pol. forms: **kudasaimasu**, etc.)
esa	food (for animals), feed
inu	dog
sangyō	industry
shorui	document
techō	diary, personal notebook

FLUENCY PRACTICE 62
Translate the following sentences into English:

1. Tomodachi ga kono kippu o kuremashita.
2. Konsarutanto ni atsumeta shiryō o agemashita.
3. Yoyogi (place name) Sangyō kara kono fakkusu o moraimashita.
4. Kono purezento o okusan ni agete kudasai.
5. Kore wa Shimizu-san kara itadaita shōsetsu desu.

Translate the following sentences into Japanese:

6. I gave Mr Saitō my card.
7. My friend gave me this photo.
8. I received this diary from Mr Kudō.
9. I received a telephone [call] from Mr Tsuji.
10. The cake that [your] wife gave [me] was really delicious.

Structure 63: (Verb)-ta/-nai hō ga ii ('It's best ...')

Kono hon o yoku yonda hō ga ii desu yo.
It's best/You had best read this book well.
Natsu no aida ni Nihon ni ikanai hō ga ii desu yo.
It's best/You had best not go to Japan during the summer.
Jibun no iken o sotchoku ni iwanai hō ga ii deshō.
It's probably best not to speak one's own opinion frankly.

CHECKNOTES 63

a) **Hō ga ii** after the Plain past gives the meaning 'It is best to ...', 'had better ...'. Note that the negative, 'It is best not to ...', requires the Plain present negative, where the Plain past negative may have been expected. **Yo** is often added at the end of such sentences, to add a slightly assertive tone.

b) Adding **deshō** gives the nuance 'It would be better to ...'.

c) Sometimes other adjectives are used in place of **ii** ('good', here 'best'). For example:
Denki seihin nara, Akihabara ni itta hō ga yasui deshō. ('If it's electrical products [you want], it would be cheaper to go to Akihabara.')
Shinkansen de itta hō ga hayai desu. ('It is quicker to go by Bullet Train.')

Checklist 63

denki seihin	electrical products (from **denki**, 'electricity', and **seihin**, 'product')
iken	opinion
jibun (no)	one's own
keizai taikoku	great economic country (from **keizai**, 'economy')
nara	if it is (see Structure 65)
... no aida ni	during ...
sotchoku da	frank (not so much of a virtue in Japan)
yōfuku	clothes

FLUENCY PRACTICE 63

Translate the following sentences into English:

1 Ima itta hō ga ii desɯ yo.
2 Nihon-go de hanashɨta hō ga ii deshō.
3 Nihon de wa yōfuku ga takai desɯ kara, kawanai hō ga ii desɯ yo.
4 Buchō to sore ni tsuite hanashɨta hō ga ii desɯ.
5 Nihon wa keizai taikoku ni narimashɨta kara, Nihon-go o naratta hō ga ii desɯ.

Translate the following sentences into Japanese:

6   It's best to phone.
7   It's best not to go by taxi.
8   It's best to reserve a hotel.
9   It's quicker to send a fax.
10 It's better to check that using the database.

Structure 64: ... ka mo shiremasen ('may')

Kare wa sensei <u>ka mo shiremasen</u>.
He <u>may be</u> a teacher.
Konban wain o nomu <u>ka mo shiremasen</u>.
I <u>may</u> drink wine tonight.
Sono wain wa oishii <u>ka mo shiremasen</u>.
The/That wine <u>may</u> be delicious.

CHECKNOTES 64

a) Using **ka mo shirenai** after the Plain style of verbs and adjectives adds the idea of 'may' (in the sense of 'it may be that ...'. (For the sense 'be allowed to', see Structure 54.)

b) As in the first example, **da** (which you might expect in this case after **sensei**) drops out before **ka mo shirenai**.

Checklist 64

kyanseru sareru	be cancelled (Passive of **kyanseru suru**, 'cancel')
okoru	get angry
konban	this evening
sore de	because of that
wain	wine

FLUENCY PRACTICE 64

Translate the following sentences into English:

1 Ashita mo isogashii ka mo shiremasen.
2 Wāpuro de repōto o kaku ka mo shiremasen.
3 Daijōbu datta ka mo shiremasen.
4 Kachō wa sore de okotte iru ka mo shiremasen.
5 Tori-shimari-yaku wa kaigi ni itte iru ka mo shiremasen.

Translate the following sentences into Japanese:

6 He may be the accountant.
7 I may go to Kōbe the day after tomorrow.
8 That company's shares may be expensive.
9 The conference may be cancelled.
10 [It] may rain tomorrow.

CONVERSATION 19: **Hoteru no resepⱷshon nite: chekku in**
('At the hotel reception: checking in')

Deibiddo Sⱷmisu:	Yoyaku o shⱡte oita Deibiddo Sⱷmisu desⱷ.
Uketsuke no hⱡto:	Hai, honjitsu kara 5(go)-haku no go-yotei de, go-yoyaku itadaite orimasⱷ. Kochira ni o-namae to go-jūsho o go-kinyū kudasai.
Deibiddo Sⱷmisu:	Kore de yoroshii desⱷ ka.
Uketsuke no hⱡto:	Hai, kekkō de gozaimasⱷ. Kochira ni sain o o-negai itashimasⱷ.
Deibiddo Sⱷmisu:	Hai.
Uketsuke no hⱡto:	O-heya wa 1012(ichi-zero-ichi-ni)-gōshitsu de gozaimasⱷ. Kochira ga kagi de gōzaimasⱷ.
Deibiddo Sⱷmisu:	Dōmo arigatō.

David Smith:	I'm David Smith. I have a reservation.
Receptionist:	Yes, we have a reservation starting today for five nights. Please fill in your name and address here.
David Smith:	Is this all right?
Receptionist:	Yes, that's fine. Please sign here.
David Smith:	O.K.
Receptionist:	Your room is number 1012. These are your keys.
David Smith:	Thank you.

Notes on Conversation 19

a) When **oku** (literally, 'put') is placed after the **-te** form it gives the nuance 'do something in preparation for'. For example: **Yoyaku o shⱡte oita Deibiddo Sⱷmisu desⱷ** (literally, 'I am David Smith who made a reservation [as a preparation]').

b) **-haku** is a counter for nights stayed. Note: 1 **ippaku**, 3 **sanpaku**, 6 **roppaku**, 8 **happaku**, 10 **juppaku (jippaku)**.

c) In **go-yoyaku itadaite orimasⱷ** ('we have received your reservation'), **-te oru** is Hum. for **-te iru**. Here it corresponds to a perfect tense in English ('have received', rather than 'are receiving').

d) In **go-kinyū kudasai, go- ... kudasai** with the stem of **suru** verbs makes a polite command.

e) **Kore de yoroshii desu ka** means 'Is this all right?' (literally, 'Is it all right with this?'). **Yoroshii** is Pol. for **ii** ('good', 'all right').

f) In an expression such as **kochira ga kagi de gozaimasu, ga** may be used, rather than **wa**, when the question 'which one?' or 'who?' is expressed or when something makes its first appearance in the conversation.

g) New words:
kinyū suru   fill in/out (a form)

go-jūsho   Hon. for **jūsho** address
go-yotei   Hon. for **yotei** schedule
honjitsu   more formal than **kyō** today
kekkō da   all right
o-heya   Hon. for **heya** room

CONVERSATION 20: Takushī
('Taxi')

Deibiddo Sumisu: Anō ... Shinjuku no Marubishi Hoteru e o-negai shimasu.
Unten-shu: Shinjuku no Marubishi Hoteru desu ne.
Deibiddo Sumisu: Ikura gurai kakarimasu ka.
Unten-shu: Daitai ¥1,000 (sen'en) gurai desu.
Deibiddo Sumisu: Ja, o-negai shimasu.
Unten-shu: Hai. ... Nihon-go ga jōzu desu ne. Doko de naratta n desu ka.
Deibiddo Sumisu: Igirisu no Nihon-go gakkō desu.
Unten-shu: Taishita mon da ne. Watashi wa gaijin-san na node dō shiyō ka to omotte ita n desu. Tasukatta.
Deibiddo Sumisu: Shikashi kyō wa atsui desu ne.
Unten-shu: Kotoshi wa atsui hi ga tsuzuite unzari shimasu yo ... Hai, tsukimashita. ¥1,200 (sen-ni-hyaku-en) desu.
Deibiddo Sumisu: Ja, ¥2,000 (ni-sen'en) de otsuri o o-negai shimasu.
Unten-shu: Hai, ¥800 (happyaku-en) no okaeshi desu.
Deibiddo Sumisu: Dōmo.

David Smith: *Er ... Please take me to the Marubishi Hotel in Shinjuku.*
Driver: *The Marubishi Hotel in Shinjuku?*
David Smith: *How much will it cost?*
Driver: *About ¥1000.*
David Smith: *All right.*
Driver: *Yes. ... You're good at Japanese. Where did you learn it?*
David Smith: *At a Japanese language school in the U.K.*
Driver: *That's really something. I was wondering what to do when I saw it was a foreigner. That was lucky.*
David Smith: *(But) today is hot, isn't it? ...*
Driver: *This year the hot days are following on and one gets fed up [with them] ... We're here. That will be ¥1,200.*
David Smith: *Please give me change from ¥2,000.*
Driver: *That's ¥800 change.*
David Smith: *Thanks.*

Notes on Conversation 20

a) In **Igirisu no Nihon-go gakkō desu̜**, **desu̜** is used to replace **de naraimashı̇ta**, which is understood.

b) **Taishı̇ta mon da ne** means 'That's impressive (isn't it?)' The remark is in the Plain form, as the driver is directing it to himself. **Taishı̇ta** ('impressive') always precedes the noun. **Mon(o)** literally means 'thing'.

c) **Na node = da kara.** Da becomes **na** before **node** ('so') and **noni** ('although').

d) **Watashi wa, gaijin-san na node dō shiyō ka to omotte ita n desu̜** means 'I was thinking it's a foreigner, (so) what shall I do?'

e) **Tasu̜katta** means 'Thank goodness!' It is related to **tasu̜keru** ('help [somebody]').

f) **Ja, ¥2,000 de otsuri o-negai shimasu̜** means 'In that case, please give me change from ¥2,000' (literally, 'In that case, it's ¥2,000 and please give me the change').

g) **...en no o-kaeshi desɰ** means 'Here is your change; ... Yen'.

h) New words:

kakaru	cost (of money); take (of time)
tsuzuku	(something) continues
unzari suru	be fed up with, have enough of
daitai	about (reinforces **gurai**, 'about', here)
gaijin	foreigner
kotoshi	this year
okaeshi	Pol. of **otsuri** change
shikashi	but, however (emphasizes the remark here)

CONVERSATION 21: Jiko shōkai
('Introducing yourself')

Deibiddo Sɰmisu: Roiyaru Fānichā no Deibiddo Sɰmisu to mōshimasɰ. Yushutsu-ka ni tsutomete orimasɰ. Nihon ni kita no wa hajimete desɰ. Dōzo yoroshɨku o-negai shimasɰ.

David Smith: *I am David Smith from Royal Furniture. I am working in the export section. It's the first time I've come to Japan. I'm looking forward to working with you.*

Notes on Conversation 21

a) **Nihon ni kita no wa hajimete desɰ** means 'It's the first time I've been (literally, 'come') to Japan'. **No wa** makes **Nihon ni kita** into the topic of the sentence. Literally, it means: '(My) having come to Japan is the first time'.

b) New words:

tsutomeru	work (takes **ni**, not **de**, to indicate place)
hajimete	the first time

CONVERSATION 22: Shiri-ai ni tsuite hanasu
('Talking about a mutual acquaintance')

Deibiddo Sᵤmisu:	Mochizuki-san o gozonji desᵤ ka.
Nakamura:	Doko ni tsutomete iru kata desᵤ ka.
Deibiddo Sᵤmisu:	Marubishi Shōji no Mochizuki-san desᵤ.
Nakamura:	Yoku shitte imasᵤ.

David Smith: Do you know Mr Mochizuki?
Nakamura: Where does he work?
David Smith: (He's Mr Mochizuki from) Marubishi Trading.
Nakamura: I know him well.

Notes on Conversation 22

a) New words:

gozonji da	Hon. of **shitte iru** know
shōji	trading

CONVERSATION 23: Yūbin-kyoku nite: kitte o kau
('At the post office: buying stamps')

Deibiddo Sᵤmisu:	Kono tegami to e-hagaki san-mai o Igirisu e okuritai n desu ga ...
Kauntā no hᵢto:	1(Ichi)-mai ¥130 (hyaku-san-jū-en) desᵤ kara, zenbu de ¥520 (go-hyaku-ni-jū-en) ni narimasᵤ. (*He hands her the money*) ... Hai, ¥1,000 (sen'en) o-azukari shimasᵤ. ¥480 (Yon-hyaku-hachi-jū-en) no okaeshi desᵤ. (*She hands him the change.*) Arigatō gozaimashᵢta.

David Smith: I'd like to send this letter and three postcards to the U.K., please.
Person at counter: They're ¥130 each, so that comes to ¥520 in all. ... ¥1,000 and ¥480 change. Thank you very much.

Notes on Conversation 23

a) **Ni narimasɰ** (literally, 'becomes') is often used as the Polite form of **da**, particularly when money or times are involved.

b) New words:
   azukaru   receive (of money)

   kauntā   counter

CONVERSATION 24: Yūbin-kyoku nite: kozutsumi o okuru
('At the post office: sending a parcel')

David doesn't want to have to pay excess luggage charges at Narita, so he goes to the post office to send non-essential items home.

Deibiddo Sɰmisu: Kono kozutsumi o Igirisu e okuritai n desu ga ...

Kauntā no hɨto: (*weighs the parcel*) Hai, 9(kyū)-kiro 500(go-hyaku)-gɰramu desɰ kara, ¥8,750 (hassen-nana-hyaku-go-jū-en) ni narimasɰ. ... Hai, ¥10,000 (ichi-man'en) no o-azukari desɰ. ¥1,250 (Sen-ni-hyaku-go-jū-en) no okaeshi desɰ. Arigatō gozaimashɨta.

David Smith: I want to send this parcel to the U.K. ...
Person at counter: Yes, it's 9 kilos and 500 grams, so that comes to ¥8,750. ... ¥10,000 and ¥1,250 change. Thank you very much.

Notes on Conversation 24

a) **... no o-azukari desɰ** means literally 'it's a receipt of ...': another Humble way of saying 'I've received ...'.

b) New words:
   -gɰramu   counter for grams
   -kiro   counter for kilograms. Note: 6 **rokkiro**, 10 **jukkiro (jikkiro)**

CONVERSATION 25: **Denwa de hoteru o yoyaku suru**
('Reserving a hotel room by phone')

Uketsuke no hito: Moshimoshi, Shirai Hoteru de gozaimasɰ.
Deibiddo Sɰmisu: Jū-yokka ni hitoban tomaritai n desu ga, furo-
tsuki no hitori-beya wa arimasɰ ka.
Uketsuke no hito: Shōshō o-machi kudasai. ... Hai, gozaimasɰ.
Ippaku ¥9,500 (kyū-sen-go-hyaku-en) to
narimasɰ. O-namae no hō wa nan to
osshaimasɰ ka.
Deibiddo Sɰmisu: Deibiddo Sɰmisu desɰ. Sɰperu wa namae ga
dī, ē, bui, ai, dī de, myōji ga esu, emu, ai, tī,
eichi desu ne.
Uketsuke no hito: Itsu-goro go-tōchaku nasaimasɰ ka.
Deibiddo Sɰmisu: Tabun 5(go)-ji-han-goro ni naru to omoimasu
ga ...
Uketsuke no hito: De wa, jū-yokka ni o-machi shite orimasɰ.

Receptionist: Hello, Shirai Hotel.
David Smith: I'd like to stay one night on the 14th. Have you
a single room with bath?
Receptionist: Just a moment. ... Yes, we have. It's ¥9,500 a
night. What is your name?
David Smith: I'm David Smith. My first name's spelled D-A-
V-I-D and my surname's spelled S-M-I-T-H.
Receptionist: What time will you be arriving?
David Smith: I think it will be about half past five.
Receptionist: We'll be expecting you on the 14th, then.

Notes on Conversation 25

a) In **O-namae no hō wa** ('As far as your name is concerned'),
no hō adds little except to make the reference to 'your name'
more indirect.

b) New words:

go-tōchaku nasaru	Hon. of **tōchaku suru** arrive
o-machi shite oru	Hum. of **matte iru** be waiting
... to naru = ... ni naru	(literally, 'becomes') is
-ban	counter for nights stayed. Note: 1 **hitoban**, 2 **futaban**

furo	bath; **furo-tsuki** with bath
-goro	about (with times)
hitori-beya	single room (from **hitori**, 'one person', and **heya**, 'room')
myōji	surname
namae	first name (often refers to first name and surname)
-nin	counter for people. Note: 1 **hitori**, 2 **futari**, 4 **yonin**, 7 **shichinin**, 9 **kunin**
superu	spelling

CONVERSATION 26: Denwa de hikō-ki no kakunin o suru
('Confirming your flight by phone')

Sha'in: Moshimoshi, Eikoku Kōkū de gozaimasu.

Deibiddo Sumisu: Watashi wa Deibiddo Sumisu to mōshimasu ga, 19 (jū-ku)-nichi ni Rondon e kaeru tsumori desu. Zaseki no konfāmu o shitai n desu ga ...

Sha'in: Hai, BA708 (bī ē nana zero hachi) desu ne. O-zaseki kakunin itashimashita.

Employee: Hello. British Airways.

David Smith: My name is David Smith. I'm intending to go back to London on the 19th. I'd like to confirm my seat.

Employee: Yes, that's BA708, isn't it? It's confirmed.

Notes on Conversation 26

a) Used after a Plain style verb, **tsumori da** adds the meaning 'intend to'.

b) Note that **o** (object) is often omitted in the set phrase **O-zaseki kakunin itashimashita** ('I have confirmed [Hum.] your seat').

c) New words:

konfāmu o suru =	
kakunin (o) suru	confirm
Eikoku Kōkū	British Airways (from **Eikoku** = **Igirisu**, 'U.K.', and **kōkū**, 'aviation')
o-zaseki	Hon. for **zaseki** seat

INFORMATION: Where do I go from here?

Language
There are many books for absolute beginners in Japanese, fewer for intermediate students and very few for advanced learners.

If you have found the incremental approach used in *Japanese For Business* helpful, you may wish to move on to *Shin-Nihongo no Kiso*, edited by the Association of Overseas Technical Scholarship, published by 3A Corporation (**Surī Ē Nettowāku**) in 1990. There are two volumes available in romanization or Japanese script (with pronunciation indicated in **hiragana**, so you do not need to know any **kanji** to use it).

Also useful is *A Dictionary of Basic Japanese Grammar*, by Seiichi Makino and Michio Tsutsui, published by the Japan Times in 1989. The examples are given in romanization and Japanese script.

Learning Japanese script
Written Japanese actually consists of three scripts: **hiragana**, **katakana** and **kanji** (originally used to write Chinese). There are 46 each of the **hiragana** and **katakana**, and 1,945 officially approved **kanji**. The number of **kanji** is certainly daunting for the beginner, but it is important to remember that the **kanji** are closely interrelated and stressing this enormously reduces the effort required to learn them.

Most people start by learning **hiragana**. If you learn 11 or 12 **hiragana** a week, within a month you will be able to write the whole Japanese language, except foreign words. This is where the **katakana** comes into the picture. The most common use of **katakana** these days is to write words borrowed from Western languages including English. It is also used for writing onomatopaeia and the names of many plants and animals and in telegrams.

There are several books for learning **kana** (**hiragana** and **katakana** collectively), but the best, in my opinion, is *Kana made easy* by Kunihiko Ogawa, published by the Japan Times (ISBN 4-7890-0517-8). The reason this book has the edge on the competition is that it makes extensive use of mnemonic aids (each **kana** letter is associated with something that has some connection to the pronunciation of the letter).

At this point, then, about eight weeks after starting (if you learnt the **katakana** at the same rate as the **hiragana**), you can now write the whole Japanese language including Western words. So why learn 1,945 **kanji**?

In the same way that English borrowed a lot of advanced vocabulary from Latin and Greek, Japanese borrowed many words from classical Chinese. There were many Chinese sounds which did not exist in Japanese (including the tones used when pronouncing Chinese, you will be pleased to know), and so sometimes as many as twenty different borrowed words, all written with different characters in Chinese, ended up with the same pronunciation in Japanese. Therefore, to avoid confusion, most words of Chinese origin are still written in **kanji**. On top of this, the Japanese also came to write many native Japanese words using **kanji** with similar meanings. So the same **kanji** may have several readings depending on the context.

Again, there are several good books for learning **kanji**, but, bearing in mind the present expense of Japanese publications, *Kanji and kana* by Wolfgang Hadamitzky and Mark Spahn, published by Tuttle (ISBN 0-8048-1373-6) would seem to be the best. It will fit conveniently in your bag, and, if you are serious about learning **kanji**, you should take it round, recycling any waste time (for example, waiting) during your day.

UNIT EIGHT

Here we look at endings meaning 'if', 'after', 'when', 'may/can' and 'while', and find out how to say 'be called', 'hear that' and 'it seems that'.

Structure 65: (verb/adjective)-ba ('if')

Dētabēsu o tsukae<u>ba</u>, subete wakarimasų.
If you use the database, you'll understand everything.
Mushi-atsu<u>kereba</u> kūrā o tsukemashō.
If it's humid, let's put the air-conditioner on.
Sono yari-kata ga benri <u>nara</u>, watashi ni mo oshiete kudasai.
If that way of doing it is convenient, please tell me (how to do it) too.
Ōta-san <u>nara</u>, dekiru to omoimasų.
If it's Mr Ohta, I think he'll be able to do it.

CHECKNOTES 65

a) Clauses ending in **-ba** are used to indicate conditions.
   Nearly always, **-ba** corresponds to 'if' in English.

   Consonant verbs replace **-u** with **-eba: hanaS.u → hanaS.eba**.

   Vowel verbs replace **-ru** with **-reba: tabE.ru → tabE.reba**.

b) **Da** has the form **nara**. Note that there is no **-ba**!
   Suru has the form **sureba**.
   Kuru has the form **kureba**.

c) **I** adjectives change **-i** to **-kereba: shirO.i → shirO.kereba**.

d) **Na** adjectives change **da** to **nara: shizuka da → shizuka nara**.

e) **Kana** and **kashira**, attached to the Plain form of verbs or adjectives, indicate the idea 'I wonder if ...'. Men use **kana** and women **kashira**. For example: **Mō itta kana** ('I wonder if he's already gone' – man speaking).

Checklist 65

oshieru	teach; tell
renshū suru	practise
tori ni kuru	come and get (from **toru**, 'take/get', and **kuru**, 'come')
ugoku	(something) moves; (a machine) works
-go ni	in ... time (follows time counter)
henji	reply
ima sugu	immediately (literally, 'now straight away')
kūrā	air-conditioner (literally, 'cooler')
ni de mo	to ... or somewhere (follows noun)
otoko	man
sae	only (follows noun)
subete	everything (adverb)

FLUENCY PRACTICE 65

Translate the following sentences into English:

1 Kikai no tsukai-kata ga wakareba, oshiete kudasai.
2 Jikan sae areba, Kamakura ni de mo iku tsumori desɯ.
   ([Plain verb] **tsumori da** = 'intend to [verb]'.)
3 Otoko nara 'kashira' de wa nakɯte, 'kana' to iimasɯ.
4 Densha de ikeba, takɯshī yori hayakɯte yasui kashira.
5 Ima sugu hitsuyō nara, juppun-go ni tori ni kite kudasai.

Translate the following sentences into Japanese:

6 If [it]'s cheap, [I]'ll buy it.
7 The machine works if [you] push this button.
8 If [you] send a fax, the reply may come the next day.
9 If [you] need [it] (use **hitsuyō da**, 'be necessary'), [I]'ll give you the report.
10 If [you] practise more, [you]'ll get better at kanji.

Structure 66: (verb/adjective)-nakereba ('if not'); (verb)-nakereba naranai ('have to')

Ima sugu ikanakereba, maniawanai deshō.
If we, etc. don't go now, we won't make it/be in time.
Sono shōhin ga takaku nakereba, kaimashō.
If that product isn't expensive, let's buy it.
Ima sugu hitsuyō de nakereba, ashita ni shimashō.
If it isn't necessary/you don't need it immediately, let's make it tomorrow.
Kanji o shikkari to benkyō shinakereba narimasen.
One, etc. must study one's kanji properly.

CHECKNOTES 66

a) The negative of the **-ba** form is made by replacing the **-nai** of the Plain negative form of verbs and adjectives with **-nakereba**. For example: **iK.a.nai** → **iK.a.nakereba** ('if I, etc. don't go'); **shirO.ku nai** → **shirO.ku nakereba** ('if it, etc. isn't white'). The negative **-ba** form of **da** ('be', etc.) is **de nakereba** ('if it isn't', etc.). Negative **-ba** forms of adjectives are not used often.

b) 'Have to' and 'must' are expressed by using phrases with **-nakereba naranai**. This literally means 'if I, etc. don't do it, it won't do', but it is best to think of it as one structure meaning 'have to'.

   This structure tends to produce very long forms which are often tongue-twisters. For example, **hatarakanakereba narimasen deshita** ('I had to work'). It is a useful structure, so it is important to get to the stage where you can pronounce the forms without stumbling!

c) **-nakereba ikenai** has much the same meaning as **-nakereba naranai**, but the degree of obligation feels slightly greater.

d) Remember that the Plain present negative of the verb **aru** ('be', etc.) is the adjective **nai**. As one would expect, the **-ba** form of **nai** is **nakereba** ('if there isn't', 'if you haven't', etc.) For example: **Jikan ga nakereba, asoko de kantan ni tabemashō** ('If there isn't time, let's have a simple meal [literally, 'eat simply'] over there').

Checklist 66

doryoku suru	make an effort
maniau	be in time ('for' is **ni**)
made ni	by (of a deadline; **roku-ji-han made ni** by half past six)
shikkari to	properly
tomo:	**futari-tomo** both of us/you, etc.; **san-nin-tomo** all three of us/you, etc.
zannen da	it's a pity

FLUENCY PRACTICE 66

Translate the following sentences into English:

1 Ganbaranakereba narimasen.
2 Futari-tomo doryoku shinakereba narimasen.
3 Zannen desu ga, yamenakereba naranai to omoimasu.
4 Isoganakereba, densha ni maniawanai deshō.
5 Mō sukoshi (a little longer, literally, 'a little more') matanakereba naranai ka mo shiremasen.

Translate the following sentences into Japanese:

6 We have to go now.
7 [You] will have to speak in Japanese.
8 If the price isn't expensive, I'll buy [them].
9 I have to write the report by Friday.
10 I may have to work tomorrow.

Structure 67: (verb/adjective)-tara ('after', 'if'); (verb)-tara ii ('should')

Sono gamen ga detara, 'jikkō' o oshite kudasai.
After that screen has appeared, please press 'Execute'.
Sono resutoran ga oishikattara, mō ichi-do ikimashō.
If that restaurant is good (literally, 'delicious'), let's go again.
Soko ga kirei dattara, shashin o ichi-mai torimashō.
If it's beautiful there (literally, 'if there is beautiful'), let's take a (literally, 'one [sheet]') photo.
De wa, sono hon o tsukattara ii deshō ka.
In that case, should I, etc. use that book?

Yokattara, kore o dōzo.
Please have this, if that's all right.
Ja, denwa shitara ...
Well, why don't you phone? (informal)
Dō shitara ii desu ka.
What should I do?

CHECKNOTES 67

a) **-tara** at the end of the first clause of a sentence indicates that the first clause occurs before the second. With verbs, this usually corresponds to 'after' or 'if' in English. With adjectives, **-tara** usually corresponds to 'if', sometimes with an idea of asking permission.

b) Note that the **-ba** form corresponds to 'if' when the idea of the first clause being a condition is stressed, wheras the **-tara** form only corresponds to 'if' when the second clause occurs after the first.

c) The **-tara** form is made simply by attaching **-ra** to the Plain past forms of verbs (see Structures 39 and 47) and adjectives (see Structures 43, 45, 50 and 52). For example:
hanaSH.i.ta → hanaSH.i.tara
hanaS.a.nakatta → hanaS.a.nakattara
omoshirO.katta → omoshirO.kattara
(omoshiO.ku nakatta → omoshirO.ku nakattara) (rare)
kirei datta → kirei dattara
(kirei de wa nakatta → kirei de nakattara) (rare)

d) **-tara ii** is a structure meaning 'should' (literally, 'If I do it, it will be all right').

e) Note that **dō** (literally, 'how') is used with **suru** ('do'), to mean 'what', unless some specific action is being considered, in which case **nani o** (literally, 'what', object) is used.

Checklist 67

renraku suru	contact (object indicated by **ni**)
shiraseru	let (somebody indicated by **ni**) know (something indicated by **o**)
shusseki suru	attend (object indicated by **ni**)
tsūjiru	get through (on the phone, etc.)

jikkō	'execute' (a key on a Japanese computer)
junbi	preparations; **junbi ga dekiru** be ready
kawari ni	instead of you, etc.; e.g. **shachō no kawari ni shusseki suru** ('attend instead of the company president')

FLUENCY PRACTICE 67
Translate the following sentences into English:

1 Igirisu ni kaettara, Kⱳrāku-san (Mr Clarke) ni renraku shimasⱳ.
2 Yatte mitara, omotta hodo muzukashɨku arimasen deshɨta.
3 Yokattara, watashi ga kawari ni yarimasⱳ.
4 Junbi ga dekitara, Tamura-san ni shirasete kudasaimasen ka.
5 Tsūjinakattara, ato de mō ichi-do kakemasⱳ.

Translate the following sentences into Japanese:

6 Please phone [me] as soon as you've arrived in Japan.
7 When the work is finished, won't [you] have a drink?
8 I will enter Kanazawa Trading (=**Shōji**) after graduating.
9 If you meet Mrs Yamada, please give her [my] card.
  (For 'give', use **watasu**, 'hand'.)
10 If [we]'re in time, let's get (**ni noru**) the 7.17 train.

Structure 68: (Plain verb/adjective) + to ('when')

Dētabēsu o tsukau <u>to</u>, Nihon no koto ga kuwashɨku wakarimasⱳ.
When/If one uses databases, one understands Japanese things in detail.
Migi e magaru <u>to</u>, tsukiatari ni kōban ga miemasⱳ.
When one turns right, one can see a police post at the end.
Akai ranpu ga tsuku <u>to</u>, kikai ga ugoki-hajimemasⱳ.
When the red light comes on, the machine starts to work.

CHECKNOTES 68
a) The Plain present plus **to** corresponds to 'when' or 'if' in English. **To** implies that the first clause triggers the second clause. It is also used when the situation described is going on in front of one's eyes, for example, when giving directions.

b) In spoken Japanese, **to** cannot be used if the verb in the second clause is in the past tense.

Checklist 68

magaru	(something) turns
mieru	is visible; can see (takes **ni**, not **de**, to indicate place)
okureru	be late; **jikan ni okureru** be late (literally, 'for a time')
ugoki-hajimeru	start to work (from **ugoku**, 'move', 'work', and **hajimeru**, 'start')
wataru	cross
byōin	hospital
de-guchi	exit (from **deru**, 'go out', and **kuchi**, 'mouth')
hayame ni	on the early side, early
hidari	left; **hidari-gawa** left-hand side
kaisū-ken	booklets of tickets (for commuting, etc.)
kōban	police post
kōshū denwa	public telephone
kyoka	permission
migi	right; **migi-gawa** right-hand side
-pēji	counter for pages. Note: 1 **ippēji**, 10 **juppēji** (**jippēji**)
ranpu	lamp, light
shingō	traffic lights
tsukiatari	end (of a street, etc.)

FLUENCY PRACTICE 68
Translate the following sentences into English:

1 Migi e magaru to, shingō ga miemasɯ.
2 Kyoka ga nai to, dekinai to omoimasɯ.
3 Nihon ni iku to, Nihon-go ga jōzu ni naru to omoimasɯ.
4 Kono repōto o yomu to, sono jiko no gen'in ga wakarimasɯ.
5 Hayame ni junbi o shite okanai to, jikan ni okuremasɯ.

Translate the following sentences into Japanese:

6 When [you]'ve crossed the road, [you]'ll see the hospital (the hospital will be visible).

7 [It]'s cheaper and more convenient if [you] buy booklets of tickets.

8 When [you]'ve arrived at the station's exit, there's a public telephone on the left(-hand side).

9 [You]'ll understand when [you]'ve read page 30 in the manual.

10 I think it takes about 12 hours, when [you] go by plane.

Structure 69: Potential verbs

Kono zasshi o itadak_emasu ka.
May I have (literally, 'receive', Hum.) this magazine?
Kono kamera no shūri ga dekimasu ka.
Can you fix this camera?

CHECKNOTES 69

a) Potential verbs are a less formal way of expressing 'can' and 'be able' than by using **-u koto ga dekiru** (Structure 38). Potential verbs are formed as follows:

Consonant verbs change **-u** to **-eru**. For example:
hanaS.u → hanaS.eru.
Note: **matsu → materu**.

Vowel verbs change **-ru** to **-rareru**. For example:
tabE.ru → tabE.rareru.

In informal speech, many young people form the Potential by adding **-reru** (instead of **-rareru**) to Vowel verbs. This is considered substandard.

b) With Potential verbs, the object was traditionally indicated with **ga**. Nowadays both **o** and **ga** are used.

c) Verbs ending in **suru** change **suru** to **dekiru**. Their objects may be indicated with **o**, for example: **Kono kamera o shūri dekimasu ka**, but more commonly **no** and **ga** are used: **Kono kamera no shūri ga dekimasu ka** (literally, 'Are you able to do a fixing of this camera?').

Checklist 69

shūri suru   fix

FLUENCY PRACTICE 69
Translate the following sentences into English:

1   O-sake wa nomemasɰ ka.
2   O-hashi o tsukaemasɰ ka.
3   Nihon-go de denwa ga kakeraremasɰ ka.
4   Kɰrejitto kādo de haraemasɰ ka.
5   Hiragana to katakana wa* kakemasu ga, kanji wa*
    kakemasen.

* Here, **wa** marks the object in both clauses. This is known as
'contrasting **wa**'.

Translate the following sentences into Japanese:

6   Can [you] swim?
7   Can [you] read Japanese?
8   Can [you] eat sushi?
9   Can [you] go to tomorrow's party?
10 Can [you] drive a car in Japan?

Structure 70: (verb)-nagara ('while')

**Kare wa sono dētabēsu o kensaku shinagara, shiryō o
atsumete imasɰ.**
He is collecting materials/information, <u>while</u> he searches that
database.

CHECKNOTES 70
a) (Verb 1)-**nagara**, (verb 2) indicates two actions occurring
    simultaneously. It usually translates as 'I, etc. (verb 2), while
    (or as) I, etc. (verb 1)' or 'I, etc. (verb 2), (verb 1)-ing'. In
    Japanese, the main action is always expressed by the second
    verb.

b) In this structure, -**nagara** is attached to the **masɰ** stem (the stem
    left when -**masɰ** is removed). Note that **da** has the irregular
    form, **de arinagara**.

c) (Verb)-**te shimau** emphasizes the preceding verb, usually
with a sense of regret. In colloquial speech it contracts to
(verb)-**chau**, or (verb)-**jau** if the **-te** form of the verb ends in
-**de**. For example:

Kanojo wa mō kaetchatta. ('She's already gone home.')
**Boku wa kinō no ban tomodachi to wisukī o zenbu
nonjatta yo**. ('I [man speaking] drank all the whisky with a
friend yesterday evening.')

Checklist 70

hiku	pull; use (of dictionary, etc.)
kangaeru	think, consider
kensaku suru	search (a database, etc.)
shokuji o suru	have a meal
sōsa suru	operate (machine)
chōsa	survey
kasa	umbrella
memo	notes, memo
ongaku	music
tokkyo	patent

FLUENCY PRACTICE 70
Translate the following sentences into English:

1 Ongaku o kikinagara, terebi o mite imashita.
2 Kanojo wa densha ni norinagara, kanji o benkyō shimashita.
3 Denwa de hanashinagara, konpyūtā o sōsa shite imashita.
4 Eigo de kangaenagara, Nihon-go o hanashite imashita kara,
baka na koto o itte shimaimashita.
5 Jisho o hikinagara, Nihon-go no tokkyo o yonde imashita.

Translate the following sentences into Japanese:

6 I write letters while [I] watch television.
7 I was speaking with the department head as [I] drank the
whisky.
8 The consultant was writing his report as [he] was doing a
survey.
9 Won't [you] speak [to me] over a meal (while we have a meal)?
10 We went [there] looking at a map, so it took a long (use
zuibun, 'extremely') time [to get there].

Structure 71: to yuu ('be called')

Watashi wa Tōmasu Mirā to iimasψ.
I am called Thomas Miller
Watakψshi wa Erizabesu Bψrakku to mōshimasψ.
I (Hum.) am called (Hum.) Elizabeth Black.
'Hirabari' to yuu machi e ikimashita.
I, etc. went to a place called 'Hirabari'.

CHECKNOTES 71

a) Apart from meaning 'say that ...' (Structure 68), **to yuu** may also correspond to 'be called ...', or just to inverted commas in English.

b) The Humble of **yuu** is **mōsu**; the Honorific is **ossharu** (irregular Polite forms: **osshaimasψ, osshaimashita**, etc.).

Checklist 71

bin	bottle
kankyō	environment

FLUENCY PRACTICE 71

Translate the following sentences into English:

1 Watakψshi wa 'Erikku Jōnzu' to mōshimasψ.
2 'Murakami-san' to yuu kata ga imasψ.
3 'Kankyō Mondai' to yuu repōto o kakimashita.
4 'Bin' wa dō yuu imi desψ ka. 'Bottle' to yuu imi desψ.
5 'Kekkyoku' wa Eigo de nan to iimasψ ka. 'Eventually' desψ.

Translate the following sentences into Japanese:

6 I'm called Sarah White (**Sērā Howaito**).
7 What does this kanji mean?
8 I met a politician called 'Tanaka'.
9 What does the 'ka' in (**no**) '**kabin**' mean? It means 'flower'.
10 How do [you] say 'environmental problem' in Japanese? [You] say '**kankyō mondai**'.

Structure 72: (Plain style) + sō desψ ('hear that ...')

> Rainen no san-gatsu ni sono hon no atarashii han ga deru <u>sō</u> <u>desψ</u>.
> <u>I hear that</u> the new edition of that book will come out in March next year.

CHECKNOTES 72
a) The Plain style plus **sō desψ** at the end of a clause indicates the idea 'I hear that ...' or 'It is rumoured ...'.

Checklist 72

kenka suru	quarrel
-gatsu	suffix indicating the month of the year. January is **ichi-gatsu** ('first month'), etc. Note: **shigatsu** April, **shichigatsu** July, and **kugatsu** September.
han	edition
hinshitsu	quality of a product
naka ga ii	get on well (of people)
shigoto ga dekiru	the work is done/ready
shitsugyō	unemployment
shōrai	(in the) future
sō yuu	such (c.f. **kō yuu**, 'like this'; **ā yuu**, 'like that'; **dō yuu**, 'what sort of?')

FLUENCY PRACTICE 72
Translate the following sentences into English:

1 Shōrai sō yuu keikaku ga aru sō desψ.
2 Moku-yōbi made ni shigoto ga dekiru sō desψ.
3 Nihon no dētabēsu ni tsuite hon o kaite iru sō desψ.
4 Yoshida-san to kenka shite iru sō desψ.
5 Mochizuki-san to Yamamoto-san wa amari naka ga yoku nai sō desψ.

Translate the following sentences into Japanese:

6 [I] hear that exam is not very difficult.
7 [I] hear that the quality of the product is not very good.
8 Who is the consultant? [I] hear it's Mrs Baker of Baker Associates (**Bēkā Asoshiētsu**).
9 [I] hear he can speak English well.
10 [I] hear she's collecting information about British unemployment problems.

Structure 73: (Plain style) + yō desψ ('It seems that ...')

> **Sore wa misu/machigai no yō desψ.**
> That looks like a mistake.
> **Sono shiken wa muzukashii yō desψ.**
> Apparently, that exam is difficult.
> **Kanojo wa genki na yō desψ.**
> She looks well.

CHECKNOTES 73

a) Plain style plus **sō desψ** (Structure 72) is concerned with what has been heard. Plain style plus **yō desψ** is used when one has evidence (usually, but not necessarily, visual) of something. It corresponds to 'It seems that ...' or 'Apparently' in English.

b) **Da** becomes **no** before **yō desψ** after nouns, and **na** after **Na** adjectives.

Checklist 73

tenkin suru	be sent to work (in another branch of a company)
ureru	sell (as in 'a product sells well')
yopparau	get drunk **yopparatte iru** be drunk
chōsa shiryō	survey (materials)
jitsu wa	in fact, actually
misu = machigai	mistake

FLUENCY PRACTICE 73

Translate the following sentences into English:

1 Kachō wa isogashii yō desψ.
2 Kantan na yō desu ga, jitsu wa, kanari muzukashii desψ.
3 Buchō wa kanari yopparatte iru yō desψ.
4 Yoyaku no kakunin o shinakereba naranai yō desψ.
5 Atarashii seihin wa yoku urete iru yō desψ.

Translate the following sentences into Japanese:

6 It looks like rain.
7 It looks quiet.
8 That word processor seems to be broken.
9 They seem to be using Mr Kawaguchi's survey (use **chōsa shiryō**).
10 That company does not seem to be carrying out much (**amari**) R&D.

CONVERSATION 27: **Narita Kūkō nite: Nihon ni yō koso**
('At Narita Airport: Welcome to Japan')

David Smith has just walked out of customs and is looking for Mr Seki, whom he does not know.

Seki: Anō, shitsurei desu ga, Roiyaru Fānichā no Deibiddo Sʉmisu-san desʉ ka.
Deibiddo Sʉmisu: Ē, sō desʉ. Marubishi Depāto no Seki-san desu ne.
Seki: Hai, sō desʉ. Yō koso. Naga-tabi de o-tsukare deshō.
Deibiddo Sʉmisu: Ē. Tabi no tsukare de sʉkoshi jisa-boke no yō desʉ.
Seki: O-nimotsu o-mochi shimashō. Eki wa kochira no hō desʉ.

Seki: *Excuse me, but are you David Smith from Royal Furniture?*
David Smith: *Yes, I am. Are you Mr Seki from Marubishi Department Store?*
Seki: *Yes, I am. Welcome (to Japan). You must be tired after your long journey.*
David Smith: *Yes, I seem to be a little jet-lagged (literally, 'with the tiredness of the journey').*
Seki: *Let me carry your luggage. The station's over here.*

Notes on Conversation 27

a) **O-(masʉ stem)-desʉ** is another way of forming an Honorific verb. It is used by Mr Seki in **Nagatabi de o-tsukare deshō** ('You must be tired').

b) In **Eki wa kochira no hō desʉ** ('The station's over here/in this direction'), the **hō** ('side') does not add much.

c) New words:
  jisa-boke   jet-lagged (from **jisa**, 'time difference')
  naga-tabi   long journey (from **nagai**, 'long', and **tabi**, 'journey')
  tsukare   tiredness (from **tsukareru**, 'get tired')
  Yō koso   Welcome

CONVERSATION 28: **Narita Kūkō nite: Rimujin Basu no chiketto o kau**
('At Narita Airport: buying a Limousine Bus ticket')

Deibiddo Sᵾmisu: Sumimasen. Shinjuku Marubishi Hoteru e iku Rimujin Basu no nori-ba wa dochira desᵾ ka.
Tsūkō-nin: Sono doa o dete hidari ni magatta tokoro ni, basᵾ-tei ga arimasᵾ. Sono 3(san)-ban ni narande kudasai.
Deibiddo Sᵾmisu: Chiketto wa doko de kaemasᵾ ka.
Tsūkō-nin: Soko no kauntā de o-motome ni naremasᵾ.
Deibiddo Sᵾmisu: Dōmo arigatō gozaimashᵢta.

David Smith: Excuse me. Where is the stop for the Limousine Bus going to the Marubishi Hotel in Shinjuku?
Passer-by: You go out of that door, turn left and the bus stop is there. You need to queue at number 3.
David Smith: Where can I buy a ticket?
Passer-by: You can get one at the counter there.
David Smith: Thank you very much.

Notes on Conversation 28

a) **Hidari ni magatta tokoro ni** means literally, 'at a place (where) you have turned left', and so here: 'just after you've turned left'.

b) **Sono 3-ban ni** means literally, 'at that number 3', and so here means, 'at the third one (bus stop)'.

c) **O-motome ni nareru** ('you can buy') is the Potential of **o-motome ni naru** which is Hon. of **motomeru** ('seek; ask for; buy').

d) New words:

deru	(here) go out of
narabu	(somebody) lines up, queues (takes **ni**, not **de**, to indicate place)
basɯ-tei	bus stop
nori-ba	bus stop; platform
tsūkō-nin	passer-by

CONVERSATION 29: **Hoteru no resepɯshon nite: chōshoku no jikan o tazuneru**
('At the hotel reception: asking when breakfast is served')

Deibiddo Sɯmisu: Ashɨta no chōshoku wa nan-ji kara desɯ ka.
Uketsuke no hɨto: 7(Shichi)-ji kara 9(ku)-ji made de gozaimasɯ. O-shokuji wa 1(ik)-kai no kafe to 2(ni)-kai no washoku no mise no dochiraka o-sɯki na hō de, o-meshiagari itadakemasɯ.

David Smith: What time does breakfast start tomorrow?
Receptionist: It's from seven until nine. You can have your meal in the café on the ground floor or the Japanese restaurant on the first floor, whichever you like.

Notes on Conversation 29

a) **Washoku no mise** ('the Japanese restaurant') means literally, the 'Japanese food shop'. When a noun describes the following noun, the two are usually linked by **no** unless they are part of the same word.

b) **Dochiraka o-sɯki na hō de** ('in whichever you like') means literally, 'in whichever side you like (Hon.)'.

c) **O-meshiagari itadakemasɯ** ('you may eat') means literally, 'I may humbly receive your eating (Hon.)'.

d) New words:

chōshoku = asa-gohan breakfast
ikkai first floor (but corresponds to the ground floor in the U.K.!)
kafe café
washoku Japanese food

CONVERSATION 30: Hoteru no resepшshon nite: Kankō ni dekaketai n desu ga.
('At the hotel reception: I'd like to go sight-seeing.')

Deibiddo Sшmisu: Tsugi no shūmatsu ni Nikkō e ikitai n desu ga, hoteru ya densha nado no annai-sho wa kochira de itadakemasш ka.
Uketsuke no hito: Hai, shōshō o-machi kudasai. Kochira ga densha no jikoku-hyō to rosen-zu de, kochira ga Nikkō no annai panfuretto desш.

David Smith: I would like to go to Nikko next weekend. Can I get guides about hotels and trains, etc. here?
Receptionist: Yes, just a moment. This is the train timetable and route map and this is a guide pamphlet to Nikko.

Notes on Conversation 30

a) **Ni** indicates the specific time when something happens, for example: **tsugi no shūmatsu ni** ('next weekend') and **ichi-ji ni** ('at 1 o'clock'). But it is not used after some common time words such as **kyō** ('today'), **kinō** ('yesterday'), **ashita** ('tomorrow') and **itsu** ('when').

b) **Ya** ('and') is used to link nouns with the implication that there may be other things included as well. For example: **hoteru ya densha nado no infomēshon** ('information about hotels and trains, etc.'). **Nado** corresponds to 'etc'.

In **densha no jikokuhyō to rosen-zu** ('train timetables and route maps'), **to** ('and') implies 'and that is all'.

c) In **hoteru ya densha nado no infomēshon, no** corresponds to 'on' or 'about' in English, although the latter is more usually conveyed by **ni tsuite (no)** or **ni kan suru** (more formal) in Japanese.

d) In **Kochira ga densha no ...**, **ga** is used rather than **wa**, because a new subject is being introduced into the conversation.

e) New words:

annai panfuretto	guide pamphlet
infomēshon	information
kankō	sight-seeing
rosen-zu	route map
shūmatsu	weekend

CONVERSATION 31: **Denwa de au yakɯsoku o suru** ('Making an appointment on the phone')

David has received an introduction from Mr Fuji to somebody at the Nanbu Department Store; he rings the store.

Kōkan-shu: Moshimoshi. Nanbu Depāto de gozaimasu ga ...

Deibiddo Sɯmisu: Yushutsu-ka no Inoue-sama wa irasshaimasɯ ka.

Kōkan-shu: Yushutsu-ka no Inoue desu ne. Hai, shōshō o-machi kudasai.

Inoue: Moshimoshi. Inoue desu ga ...

Ending one:

Deibiddo Sɯmisu: Roiyaru Fānichā no Sɯmisu desɯ.

Inoue: A', Fuji-san kara o-hanashi o ukagatte imasɯ. Tōsha e wa itsu o-ide ni naremasɯ ka.

Deibiddo Sɯmisu: Dekimashɨtara, konshū no sui-yōbi no gogo ni o-ukagai shitai n desu ga.

Inoue: Chotto o-machi kudasai. Sui-yōbi deshɨtara, san-ji-han kara de yoroshii deshō ka.

Deibiddo Sɯmisu: Ē, sore de wa sui-yōbi no san-ji-han to yuu koto de.

Ending two:

Deibiddo Sᵤmisu: Roiyaru Fānichā no Sᵤmisu desᵤ. Chikai uchi ni o-ai dekimasᵤ ka.

Inoue: Ē, mochiron desᵤ. Itsu-goro ga go-tsugō yoroshii deshō ka.

Deibiddo Sᵤmisu: Sō desu ne. Inoue-san mo asatte no shōhin setsumei-kai ni shusseki saremasu ne. Sono ato o-jikan wa arimasᵤ ka.

Inoue: Ē. Sore de wa sono toki ni uchi-awase shimashō.

Switchboard: Hello. Nanbu Department Store.

David Smith: Is Mr Inoue in the export section there?

Switchboard: Mr Inoue in the export section? Just a moment.

Inoue: Hello. Inoue, here.

Ending one:

David Smith: This is Smith from Royal Furniture.

Inoue: Oh, I've heard about you from Mr Fuji. When can you come to see us?

David Smith: Let me see. You're attending the product demonstration tomorrow, aren't you? Have you got any time after that?

Inoue: Yes. In that case, let's discuss it then.

Ending two:

David Smith: This is Smith from Royal Furniture. Would it be possible for me to see you in the near future?

Inoue: Yes, of course. When would be convenient for you?

David Smith: If possible, I'd like to come on Wednesday afternoon this week.

Inoue: Just a moment. Would half past three on Wednesday be all right?

David Smith: Yes. In that case, half past three on Wednesday.

Notes on Conversation 31

a) In **Fuji-san kara o-hanashi o ukagatte imas** ('I've been hearing about you from Mr Fuji'), **ukagau** is the Hum. equivalent of **kiku** ('hear', 'listen'). The sentence literally means, 'I'm hearing stories about (you) from Mr Fuji.'

b) **O-ide ni naru** is an alternative Honorific equivalent of **kuru** or **iku**. The other Honorific, **irassharu**, is not used in the Potential.

c) **Dekimashitara** (more polite than **dekitara**, from **dekiru** ['be able']) is an idiom meaning 'if it is possible'.

d) **To yuu koto de** is best left untranslated here. It literally means 'with the arrangement (**koto** really means 'thing') being ...'.

e) **Mochiron** means 'of course'. **Des** makes the expression more polite: **Mochiron des**.

f) Several Polite forms are used in **Itsu-goro ga go-tsugō yoroshii deshō ka** ('When would be convenient for you?'). **-goro** is a suffix used after time expressions, meaning 'about'. Used after **itsu** ('when?'), it makes the question word politer by making it vaguer. **Yoroshii** is the Polite equivalent of **ii** ('good').

g) **Shusseki sareru** is the passive of **shusseki suru** ('attend'), but passives are often used as Honorific verbs, as here in **shusseki saremas**.

h) New words:

go-tsugo	Hon. form of **tsugō** convenience
shōhin setsumei-kai	product demonstration (from **shōhin**, 'goods', **setsumei**, 'explanation', and **kai**, 'meeting')
sono ato	after that
sono toki	then (literally, 'that time')
tōsha	this/our company
uchi-awase suru	discuss

CONVERSATION 32: **Michi o tazuneru**
('Asking the way')

Deibiddo Sɯmisu: Sumimasen, Tōkyo Eki ni wa dono yō ni shɨte ikeba ii desɯ ka.

Tsūkō-nin: Tsugi no shingō o hidari ni magatte, massugu ni iku to, ōki na hon'ya ga arimasɯ. Sono kado o migi ni magatte 500m (go-hyaku-mētoru) hodo aruku to hiroi dōro ni demasɯ. Sono michi o wataru to Tōkyō Eki no Minami-Guchi desɯ.

Deibiddo Sɯmisu: Shinkansen nori-ba mo onaji tokoro desɯ ka.

Tsūkō-nin: Ē, Minami-Guchi ni Shinkansen-yō no kaisatsu ga atta to omoimasɯ yo.

Deibiddo Sɯmisu: Dōmo arigatō gozaimashɨta.

David Smith: Excuse me. How do I get to Tokyo Station?

Passer-by: If you turn left at the next lights, and go straight ahead, there's a big book shop. If you turn right at that corner, and walk for about 500 metres, you come out into a wide road. Cross that road and you're at the South Exit of Tokyo Station.

David Smith: Are the Bullet Train platforms in the same place, too?

Passer-by: Yes, I think that there was a wicket for the Bullet Train at the South Exit.

David Smith: Thank you very much indeed.

Notes on Conversation 32

a) (Verb)-**ba ii**, as in **Tōkyo Eki ni wa dono yō ni shɨte ikeba ii desɯ ka**, is similar to (verb)-**tara ii** ('should [verb]') – see Structure 67.

b) Note that **onaji** ('same') can precede a noun without **na** or **no**. Except for this peculiarity, it behaves like a **Na** adjective.

c) New words:

deru	(here) come out on
dōro	road
kado	corner

kaisatsu	ticket barrier
massugu ni	straight ahead
Minami-Guchi	South Exit (from **minami**, 'South', and **kuchi**, 'mouth')
ōki na = ōkii	big (but **ōki na** may only be used before a noun)
tokoro	place
-yō no	for (the use of) (follows noun)

CONVERSATION 33: Ban-gohan
('Dinner')

Seki:	Anō sumimasen. O-sake 2(ni)-hon o-negai shimasṳ. (*The sake arrives.*) Kanpai!
Deibiddo Sṳmisu:	Kanpai!
Seki:	(*to the waitress*) Sumimasen. Sṳki-yaki motte kite moraemasṳ ka.
Deibiddo Sṳmisu:	(*The food arrives.*) Oishisō desu ne.
Seki:	Nihon ryōri wa o-sṳki desṳ ka.
Deibiddo Sṳmisu:	Hai, totemo sṳki desṳ. Toku ni sṳki-yaki ga sṳki desṳ ... Go-chisō-sama deshɨta. Totemo oishɨkatta desṳ.

Seki:	Er, excuse me. Two rice wines please. ... Cheers!
David Smith:	Cheers!
Seki:	Excuse me. Would you bring us some suki-yaki, please.
David Smith:	That looks good.
Seki:	Do you like Japanese food?
David Smith:	Yes, I like it very much. I'm particularly fond of suki-yaki ... Thank you for treating me. It was really delicious.

Notes on Conversation 33

a) **Sṳki-yaki motte kite moraemasṳ ka** ('Would you bring us some suki-yaki?') means literally, 'May I receive the bringing of suki-yaki?' Note how object **o** is omitted here.

173

b) **Oishisō desu ne** means 'It looks tasty, doesn't it?' Removing the 'i' from an **I** adjective and replacing it with **-sō da** gives the meaning 'looks (adj.)'.

c) Other expressions essential when eating are:
Oishii desu ne (It's delicious, isn't it?')
Oishikatta desu ne ('That was delicious, wasn't it?')
Go-chisō-sama deshita (an expression used at the end of a meal, meaning literally, 'It was a (Hon.) running-about/feast' – presumably because it is necessary to run round in order to produce a feast!)

d) New words:

motte kuru	bring (literally, 'having come'). Compare **motte iku** ('take [something] with one').
-hon	counter for bottles, pencils, trees and other cylindrical things. Note: 1 **ippon**, 3 **sanbon**, 6 **roppon**, 8 **happon**, 10 **juppon** (**jippon**); how many? = **nanbon**.
kanpai	cheers (literally, 'empty glass')
o-sᵤki desᵤ	Hon. form of **sᵤki da** like
sᵤki-yaki	Japanese grilled beef dish
toku ni	especially

CONVERSATION 34: Kagu tenji-kai no sᵤkejūru toi-awase
('Enquiring about the schedule of a furniture exhibition')

Deibiddo Sᵤmisu: Moshimoshi, Kagu Seizō Kyōkai desᵤ ka.
Jimu-in: Hai.
Deibiddo Sᵤmisu: Chijin kara tenji-kai ga aru to kiita n desu ga, kuwashᵢku oshiete itadakemasen ka.
Jimu-in: Dono tenji-kai desᵤ ka.
Deibiddo Sᵤmisu: 11(Jū-ichi)-gatsu 28(ni-jū-hachi)-nichi kara Makuhari to yuu tokoro de aru mono desᵤ.
Jimu-in: Hai, wakarimashᵢta. Sᵤkoshi o-machi kudasai. ... O-matase itashimashᵢta. 11-gatsu 28-nichi kara 12(jū-ni)-gatsu 4(yok)-ka made, mainichi asa 9(ku)-ji 30(san-jup)-pun kara yūgata 6(roku)-ji made hirakaremasᵤ. Kaijō wa Makuhari Konbenshon Sentā 1(ichi)-gōkan de, nyūjō-ryō wa hitori ¥500 (go-hyaku-en) desᵤ.
Deibiddo Sᵤmisu: Panfuretto wa arimasᵤ ka.

| *Jimu-in:* | Hai, kaijō de 1(ichi)-bu ¥200 (ni-hyaku-en) de hanbai shɨte orimasɰ. |
| *Deibiddo Sɰmisu:* | Arigatō gozaimashɨta. |

David Smith:	Hello, is that the Furniture Manufacturers' Association?
Employee:	Yes.
David Smith:	I've heard from an acquaintance that there will be an exhibition. Could you tell me more about it?
Employee:	Which exhibition is that?
David Smith:	It's being held from the 28th November at a place called 'Makuhari'.
Employee:	Oh, yes. Please wait a moment ... Sorry for keeping you waiting. It is open every day from the 28th November until the 4th December from 9.30 a.m. till 6.00 p.m. The venue is Hall 1 at Makuhari Convention Centre and the entrance fee is ¥500 per person.
David Smith:	Is there a pamphlet?
Employee:	Yes, they're being sold at the venue for ¥200 each.
David Smith:	Thank you very much.

Notes on Conversation 34

a) **Kuwashɨku oshiete itadakemasen ka** ('Could you tell me more about it?') means literally, 'Can I receive (Hum.) (you) telling (me) in detail?'

b) **Makuhari to yuu tokoro de aru mono desɰ** ('It's the one that will be held somewhere called "Makuhari"') is literally, 'It's a thing which will exist at a place which is called "Makuhari".' Note that in this usage, **aru** takes **de**, rather than **ni**, to indicate place.

c) **Sɰkoshi o-machi kudasai = Shibaraku o-machi kudasai** ('Please wait a moment').

d) **Hitori go-hyaku-en desɰ** means 'It's ¥500 for one person'.

Ichi-bu ni-hyaku-en de means 'at ¥200 for one (pamphlet, etc.).'

e) New words:

aru	be, exist; (here) happen, be held
hanbai suru	be on sale ('sell' is usually **uru**)
hirakareru	be opened (of event)
shɨte oru	Hum. of **shɨte iru** be doing/making
-bu	counter for pamphlets, etc.
chijin	acquaintance
-gōkan	counter for buildings
jimu-in	clerk
kaijō	(exhibition) hall
konbenshon	convention
kyōkai	association
nyūjo-ryō	entrance fee
seizō	manufacturing
sɰkejūru	schedule
toi-awase	enquiry

CONVERSATION 35: **Kaisha naiyō setsumei**
('Explaining what your company does')

Deibiddo Sɰmisu: Sore de wa, tōsha no gyōmu naiyō o go-setsumei sasete itadakitai to omoimasu ga, yoroshii deshō ka.

Suzuki: Hai, o-negai shimasɰ.

Deibiddo Sɰmisu: Gyōmu naiyō o matomemashɨta panfuretto ga gozaimasɰ node, sore ni sotte setsumei sasete itadakimasɰ. ... 8(Hachi)-pēji o goran kudasai. Roiyaru Fānichā wa 1850 (sen-happyaku-go-jū)-nen ni setsuritsu saremashɨta. Dentō no aru Igirisu kagu o, chūmon ni ōjite hando meido de seizō shɨte imasɰ. Jūgyō-in wa, genzai 55(go-jū-go)-nin desɰ. Honsha to shō rūmu wa Rondon ni, kōjō wa Debon ni arimasɰ. Sakunen no nenkan uri-age-daka wa 1,000,000 (hyaku-man)-pondo de, keijō rieki wa 100,000 (jū-man)-pondo deshɨta. Nanika fumei na ten wa gozaimasɰ deshō ka.

> *David Smith:* In that case, I'd like to explain what our company does. Is that all right?
> *Suzuki:* Yes. Go ahead.
> *David Smith:* There is a pamphlet with a description of what we do in it, so I'll refer to that during my explanation. ... Please turn to page 8.
> Royal Furniture was established in 1850. We manufacture traditional British furniture by hand to order. At present we have 55 employees. Our headquarters and show-room are in London and our factory is in Devon. Last year our sales were £1,000,000 and our ordinary profit was £100,000.
> Are there any points which you are not clear about?

Notes on Conversation 35

a) **(Go-) ... sasete itadaku** is a structure which makes a **suru** verb, for example **setsumei suru** ('explain'), Humble, as, for instance, in **... o go-setsumei sasete itadakitai to omoimasu ga, yoroshii deshō ka** ('I would like to explain ..., but is that all right?').

b) (Verb)-**tai to omou** literally means, 'I think that I want to (verb)'.

c) **Gyōmu naiyō o matomemashita panfuretto** means 'a pamphlet [where they] have brought together what we do'. In normal speech the Plain past (ending in **-ta**) rather than the Polite past (ending in **-mashita**) would be used in a relative clause like this. Using the Polite forms in such situations indicates a sort of 'super-polite' speech.

d) **Goran kudasai** is the imperative of **goran ni naru** ('see', Hon.).

e) Note how years are represented, in **sen-happyaku-go-jū-nen** ('1850'). **-nen** is the counter for years. Note: 4 **yonen**.

f) **Dentō no aru** ('traditional') means literally, 'which has tradition'. **Ga** is often replaced by **no** in relative clauses.

g) **Chūmon ni ōjite** ('to order') means literally, 'responding to order'.

h) **Honsha to shō rūmu wa Rondon ni ...:** Note how **atte** ('is and') is omitted after the first **ni** in this sentence.

i) In **Nanika fumei na ten wa gozaimasu̜ deshō ka** ('Are there any points which you are not clear about?'), **nanika** ('anything') adds the idea of 'any'. Unusually, **gozaru** (Hum. equivalent of **aru**) is always used in the Polite form before **deshō**.

j) New words:

fumei da	unclear
genzai	(at) present
gyōmu naiyō	what we do (from **gyōmu**, 'business', and **naiyo**, 'contents')
hando meido de	hand-made (adverb)
honsha	main office (of company)
jūgyō-in	employee
keijō rieki	ordinary profit
nenkan uri-age-daka	sales for the year
-pondo	counter for pounds. Note: 10 **juppondo** (**jippondo**)
sakunen	a formal equivalent of **kyonen** last year
seizō suru	manufacture
setsuritsu sareru	be established; Passive of **setsuritsu suru** establish
shō rūmu	show-room
sore ni sotte	according to/following that
ten	point. Note: '3.6' would be **san-ten-roku**

CONVERSATION 36: **Kono shōhin wa Nihon de yoku uresō desu̶ ka.**
('Do you think this product will sell well in Japan?')

Deibiddo Su̶misu: Kochira no tēburu wa, Eikoku de wa taihen ninki no takai seihin desu̶. Shikashi saizu wa su̶koshi ōkime na n desu ga, Nihon de mo yoku ureru to o-kangae ni narimasu̶ ka.

Ōno: Totemo utsukushii tēburu desu ne. Shikashi kono saizu wa Nihon no jūtaku ni wa shōshō ōkisugiru yō desu̶. Kono seihin ni kanshi̶te wa ōki na shijō wa kitai dekimasen ne.

Deibiddo Su̶misu: Naruhodo. Shikashi tōsha wa haba-hiroku ōku no seihin o atsukatte orimasu̶. Bu̶rōshā no naka de, nanika mikomi no aru seihin wa arimasu̶ ka.

Ōno: Ē. Kono ori-tatami-shi̶ki no tēburu nanka totemo ii desu ne. Kono yō na seihin wa Nihon de mita koto ga arimasen yo.

David Smith: This table is very popular in the U.K. However, it's a little on the large size. Do you think it would sell well in Japan too?

Ōno: It's a very beautiful table, isn't it? However, it looks a little too large for Japanese housing. We can't expect a big market for this product.

David Smith: I see. But our company is dealing in a wide range of products. Is there any product in the brochure which looks promising?

Ōno: Yes. Something like this folding table is very good, isn't it? I haven't seen anything like this product in Japan.

Notes on Conversation 36

a) **Ōkisugiru yō desu̶** means 'It looks as if it is too big'. When added to the **masu̶** stem of a verb or an adjective stem (the part left when **-i** or **da** is removed), **-sugiru** means 'too'.

b) **... ni kanshi̶te wa** means 'as far as ... is concerned'.

c) **Naruhodo** ('really') is more often sarcastic than **Sō desu̶ ka** ('Is that so?'; 'I see'), so is best avoided in the early stages.

d) **Nanka** means 'something like'. Note that **wa** is omitted.

e) **-sō da**: This suffix is attached to the **masu** stem of a verb or an adjective stem to add the meaning 'look as if'. **Kono shōhin wa Nihon de yoku uresō desu ka** means literally, 'Does it look as if this product will sell well in Japan?'

f) New words:

atsukau	deal with
burōshā	brochure
Eikoku	formal alternative to **Igirisu** U.K.
haba-hiroku	over a wide range (from **haba**, 'width', **hiroi**, 'wide', and **-ku**)
jūtaku	housing
kitai suru	expect
kochira no	Pol. form of **kono** this (followed by a noun)
kono yō na	this sort of (followed by noun)
mikomi no aru	promising (literally, 'which has promise')
ninki no takai	popular (literally, 'which has high popularity')
o-kangae ni naru	Hon. of **kangaeru** think
ōkime da	be on the big side
ōku no =	many (followed by noun)
takusan no	
ori-tatami-	foldable (from **oru**, 'fold', **tatamu**, 'fold up',
shiki (no)	and **-shiki**, 'style')
saizu	size
seihin	product
shijō	market
shōshō	Pol. equivalent of **sukoshi** a little
taihen = totemo	very
tēburu	table
utsukushii	beautiful (stronger than **kirei da**)

CONVERSATION 37: **Byōin no uketsuke nite**
('At the reception in the hospital')

Deibiddo Sumisu: O-hayō gozaimasu.

Uketsuke no hito: O-hayō gozaimasu. Nihon-go wa hanasemasu ka.

Deibiddo Sumisu: Ē, daitai nara ...

Uketsuke no hito: Dō nasaimashita?

Deibiddo Sumisu: Zutsū ga suru n desu ga.

Uketsuke no hito: Sō desɯ ka.

Deibiddo Sɯmisu: (*showing her his insurance certificate*)
Watashi no hoken ni wa iryō teate ga
fukumarete iru n desu ga, kochira de wa
atsukatte iru deshō ka.

1 Uketsuke no hito: Hai, atsukatte orimasɯ. Kochira ni
o-namae to jūsho o kaite kudasai. De wa,
shōshō o-machi kudasai.

or 2 Uketsuke no hito: Sumimasen ga, kochira de wa atsukatte
orimasen. Sakura Byōin nara, atsukatte
iru to omoimasu ga ...

David Smith: Good morning.

Receptionist: Good morning. Can you speak
Japanese?

David Smith: Yes, more or less ...

Receptionist: What's wrong with you? (Literally, 'What
did you do?' [Hon.])

David Smith: I've got a headache.

Receptionist: I see.

David Smith: Medical treatment is included in my
insurance. Do you accept this here?

1 Receptionist: Yes, we do. Please write your name and
address here. Please wait a moment.

or 2 Receptionist: I'm sorry, but we don't accept that here. I
think Sakura Hospital does accept it ...

Notes on Conversation 37

a) **Daitai nara** ('more or less') means literally, 'if it's the outline'.

b) **Sakura Byōin nara** ('If you try the Sakura Hospital') means
literally, 'if it is the Sakura Hospital'.

c) New words:

atsukau	(here) accept
fukumareru	be included; Passive of **fukumu** include
fukutsū	stomach ache
hoken	insurance
iryō teate	medical treatment
O-hayō gozaimasɯ	Good morning (literally, 'It's early' [Hum.])
sakura	cherry (tree) (from **saku**, 'bloom')

yōtsū   lumbago
zutsū   headache; **zutsū ga suru** have a headache
(more formal than **atama ga itai**)

CONVERSATION 38: Byōin nite
('At the hospital')

Deibiddo Sᵤmisu: O-hayō gozaimasᵤ.
Fujii-sensei: O-hayō gozaimasᵤ. Nihon-go de daijōbu desᵤ
ka.
Deibiddo Sᵤmisu: Daitai wakarimasᵤ.
Fujii-sensei: Dō saremashɨta?
Deibiddo Sᵤmisu: Nihon ni mikka-mae ni tsuita n desu ga, zutto
atama ga itakᵤte ...
Fujii-sensei: Ja, chotto mite mimashō. Dono hen ga
itamimasᵤ ka.
Deibiddo Sᵤmisu: Mimi no chikaku ga itai n desu ga ...
Fujii-sensei: Osoraku hikō-ki ni notta toki ni okashɨku natta
n deshō. Kore wa kusuri de kantan ni
naorimasᵤ kara, shinpai (wa) irimasen yo.
Moshi ashɨta made itami ga tsuzuku yō
deshɨtara, mō ichi-do shinsatsu o ukete
kudasai.
Deibiddo Sᵤmisu: Wakarimashɨta. Dōmo arigatō gozaimashɨta.

David Smith: Good morning.
Dr Fujii: Good morning. Is it all right to speak Japanese?
David Smith: I understand more or less.
Dr Fujii: What's wrong with you?
David Smith: I arrived in Japan three days ago, and I've had
a headache ever since ...
Dr Fujii: Well, let me just have a look at you. Where is
the pain?
David Smith: It's sore round my ears.
Dr Fujii: It probably started playing up (literally,
'became funny') when you were in the plane.
This is some medicine. It will get better easily,
so you don't need to worry. If it looks as if the
pain is going to keep on until tomorrow, please
have another examination.
David Smith: All right. Thank you very much.

Notes on Conversation 38

a) Remember that in **Nihon-go de daijōbu desꙍ ka** ('Is it all right [to speak] in Japanese?') the word for 'speak' is left out.

b) **Chotto mite mimashō** ('Let me have a look [at you]') means literally, 'Let me try looking a bit'. **Chotto** is often equivalent to 'have a ...' or adds an apologetic note.

c) Unfinished sentences ending in **-te, ga** ('but') and **shi** ('and [as if that isn't enough]') are common. For instance, **Zutto atama ga itakꙍte ...** ('I've had a headache ever since and ...').

d) **Toki (ni)** ('when') follows Plain verb and adjective forms.

e) New words:

chikaku	near (noun)
daitai	more or less
dono	which? (followed by noun)
hen	area, part
iru	be necessary (Consonant verb)
itami	pain
itamu	be painful
kusuri	medicine
-mae ni	... ago
mimi	ear
moshi	if
naoru	heal; (here) get better
osoraku	perhaps, probably
sareru	Passive of **suru** ('do'), here used as Honorific
sensei	teacher (here, Doctor)
shinpai	worry
shinsatsu	examination (at the doctor's)
ukeru	receive
zutto	all the time; (here) ever since

f) Some extra words for a visit to the dentist:

ha-isha	dentist (from **ha**, 'tooth', and **isha**, 'doctor')
kakeru	(a tooth) breaks
kꙍraun	(dental) crown
toreru	come off/out (c.f. **toru**, 'take')
tsume-mono	filling (from **tsumeru**, 'fill', and **mono**, 'thing')

Ha ga itai desꙍ. I have toothache.
Tsume-mono ga torete shimaimash꙲ta. I've lost a filling.
Kꙍraun ga torete shimaimash꙲ta. My crown has come off.
Ha ga kakete shimaimash꙲ta. I've broken a tooth.

INFORMATION: Useful addresses and publications

The following organizations are likely to be useful to you while you are planning your trip and when you are in Japan.

Information providers

Japan National Tourist Organisation
Tel: 0171-734 9638 Fax: 0171-734 4290
20 Savile Row, London, W1X 1AE

Tourist Information Center (Japan National Tourist Organization)
Tel: (03) 3502 1461
6-6, Yurakucho 1-chome, Chiyoda-ku, Tokyo 100

This telephone number may also be used in Tokyo for the Japan Travel Phone service, 'for those in need of English language assistance or travel information'. Outside Tokyo, phone 0120 222800 in eastern Japan or 0120 444800 in western Japan (toll-free) for this service.

Japanese Embassy (Japan Information and Cultural Centre)
Tel: 0171-465 6500 Fax: 0171-491 9347
101-104 Piccadilly, London W1V 9FN

British Embassy in Tokyo (Commercial Department)
Tel: (03) 3265 6340 Fax: (03) 3265 5580
1, Ichibancho, Chiyoda-ku, Tokyo 102

Department of Trade and Industry (Exports to Japan Unit)
Tel: 0171-215 4804 Fax: 0171-222 2629
7th Floor, Kingsgate House, 66-74 Victoria Street, London SW1E 6SW

Japan External Trade Organisation
Tel: 0171-493 7226 Fax: 0171-491 7570
Leconfield House, Curzon Street, London W1Y 8LQ

British Chamber of Commerce in Japan
Tel: (03) 3267 1901 Fax: (03) 3267 1903
3F Kenkyusha Eigo Centre Building, 1-2 Kagurazaka, Shinjuku-ku, Tokyo 162

British Council (Office of the Cultural Counsellor)
Tel: (03) 3235 8031
1-2 Kagurazaka, Shinjuku-ku, Tokyo 162

Buying Japan-related publications

Asahiya Bookstores
Tel. 0181-200 0039 Fax 0181-200 8872
Unit 34, Yaohan Plaza, 399 Edgware Road, London NW9 0JJ

Books Nippon
Tel. 0171-248 4956 Fax 0171-489 1171
64/66 St Paul's Churchyard, London EC4M 8AA

Japan Centre
Tel. 0171-439 8035 Fax 0171-287 1082
212 Piccadilly, London W1V 9LD

Advertising

Dentsu UK Ltd
Tel: 0171-499 9124 Fax: 0171-493 7491
Berger House, 1st Floor, 36/38 Berkeley Square, London W1X 5DA

Hakuhodo Inc.
Tel: 0171-493 5438 Fax: 0171-493 5430
14/15 Conduit Street, London W1R 9TG

Business cards

Japanese Language Services, Ltd
Tel: 0171-435 3160 Fax: 0171-435 2566
11 Fawley Road, London NW6 1SJ

Doctors, dentists and hospitals

See *Japan Yellow Pages* and *City source*.

Publications

Addresses
You can find addresses in the following publications:
Japanese addresses in the U.K., Insight Japan
Japan Yellow Pages, Japan Yellow Pages Ltd
City source: English telephone directory: Tokyo edition and Kansai edition (for Western Japan including Osaka and Kyoto), NTT et al.
Japan directory, The Japan Press Ltd
Japan company handbook, Toyo Keizai Inc., ISSN 0288-9307

Travel guide
Japan – a travel survival kit, Robert Strauss, Chris Taylor and Tony Wheeler, 1994, Lonely Planet, ISBN 0-8644-2237-7

Business guides
Signposts to Japanese technology: a practical handbook for accessing Japanese technology, InterMatrix Group, 1993
British business in Japan, P&B International

Accommodation
Hotels in Japan, Japan National Tourist Organization
Also see *Japan – a travel survival kit*, above.

Background reading
A history of modern Japan, Richard Storry, 1982, Penguin, ISBN 0-14-013512-X
Understanding Japanese society, Joy Hendry, 1995, Routledge, ISBN 0-415-10259-6
Nippon: a chartered survey of Japan, Kokuseisha (updated annually)

Unless a publication date is stated, the above publications are updated annually.

Database

Nikkei Telecom (for newspapers online and financial information)
Tel: 0171-822 0684 Fax: 0171-822 0689
Mitsui & Co., Network Services Department, 20 Old Bailey, London EC4M 7QQ

KEY TO EXERCISES

UNIT ONE

FLUENCY PRACTICE 1: 1 I, etc. am John White. 2 I, etc. am American. 3 I, etc. am a designer. 4 I, etc. am Linda Taylor. 5 I, etc. am German. 6 Sensei desψ. 7 Watto-san desψ. 8 Kaikei-shi desψ. 9 Fψransu-jin desψ. 10 Kōmu-in desψ.

FLUENCY PRACTICE 2: 1 This is a ticket. 2 That is a camera. 3 That (over there) is a plane. 4 I am Chinese. He is British. 5 I am Mark Howell. I am a lawyer. 6 Kare wa enjinia desψ. 7 Kanojo wa jānarisψto desψ. 8 Kare-ra wa seiji-ka desψ. 9 Tanaka-san wa hisho desψ. 10 Watashi-tachi wa Igirisu-jin desψ. Kare-ra wa Nihon-jin desψ.

FLUENCY PRACTICE 3: 1 This is a pen. That is also a pen. 2 She is French. We are also French. 3 This is a pencil. That (over there) is also a pencil. 4 We are consultants. They are also consultants. 5 This is a business card. That (over there) is also a business card. 6 Kare wa ten'in desψ. Kare-ra mo ten'in desψ. 7 Kanojo wa Amerika-jin desψ. Watashi-tachi mo Amerika-jin desψ. 8 Kore wa nekutai desψ. Are mo nekutai desψ. 9 Watashi wa bijinesuman desψ. Jōnzu-san mo bijinesuman desψ. 10 Are wa shāpupen desψ. Are mo shāpupen desψ.

FLUENCY PRACTICE 4: 1 She is not a writer. 2 That is not a promise. 3 This (place) is not the station. 4 He is not a banker. He is a professor. 5 That (place over there) is not a flat. 6 Kare wa tori-shimari-yaku de wa arimasen. 7 Kanojo wa Kanada-jin de wa arimasen. 8 Watashi-tachi wa shinbun kisha de wa arimasen. 9 Koko wa depāto de wa arimasen. 10 Watashi wa Amerika-jin de wa arimasen. Igirisu-jin desψ.

FLUENCY PRACTICE 5: 1 Is this a word processor? 2 Is he a businessman? 3 Isn't she Japanese? 4 Is that (place) the toilet? 5 Aren't they civil servants? 6 Sore wa repōto desψ ka. 7 Kare wa kaikei-shi desψ ka. 8 Kanojo wa Tanaka-san de wa arimasen ka. 9 Kare-ra wa Doitsu-jin de wa arimasen ka. 10 Soko wa kaisha de wa arimasen ka.

FLUENCY PRACTICE 6: 1 What's your name? I'm Michael Green. 2 What's your job? I'm a businessman. 3 What is that? It's a map.

4 Who is he? He's Mr Elliott. 5 Where is this? It's the station.
6 Kanojo wa dare desψ ka. Murayama-san desψ. 7 Kare wa
dare desψ ka. Kare wa Jon-san desψ. 8 Shachō wa donata
desψ ka. Okutsu-san desψ. 9 Koko wa doko desψ ka.
Musashino Seimitsu Kiki desψ. 10 Kanojo wa dare desψ ka.
Bēkā-san desψ.

FLUENCY PRACTICE 7: 1 It's my bag. 2 It's his passport.
3 London is the capital of the U.K. 4 Is this a map of Tokyo?
5 He is the director of Nagoya Automobiles. 6 Nihon no shushō
wa dare desψ ka. 7 Sore wa dare no meishi desψ ka. Sψmisu-
san no meishi desψ. 8 Dare no konpyūtā desψ ka. Yamaguchi-
san no desψ. 9 Kare wa Akasaka Kikai no shachō desψ ka.
10 Dare no kōto desψ ka. Kawajima-san no kōto desψ.

FLUENCY PRACTICE 8: 1 What number is it? It's 8749.
2 What's your room number? It's 574. 3 What's your phone
number? It's Tokyo 03-3745 9487. 4 Kψrejitto kādo no bangō
wa nan-ban desψ ka. Yon-go-zero-zero san-yon-kyū-hachi san-
roku-go-nana hachi-kyū-yon-ni desψ. 5 Denwa bangō wa nan-
ban desψ ka. Zero-ichi-nana-ichi san-ni-san no yon-go-nana-kyū
desψ. 6 Kagi no bangō wa nan-ban desψ ka. Go-yon-hachi-
nana-ni desψ.

FLUENCY PRACTICE 9: 1 How much are the business cards?
They're ¥5,400. 2 How much is that clock/watch? It's ¥3,300.
3 How much are those goods? They're ¥9,500. 4 How much
is that printer (over there)? It's ¥35,000. 5 How much is this
computer? It's ¥80,000. 6 O-kanjō wa ikura desψ ka. Zenbu de
kyū-sen-yon-hyaku-go-jū-en desψ. 7 Ryōkin wa ikura desψ ka.
Nana-sen-yon-hyaku-kyū-jū-en desψ. 8 Setto wa ikura desψ ka.
Ni-man-go-hyaku-en desψ. 9 Kikai wa ikura desψ ka. Hyaku-
man'en desψ. 10 Kagu wa ikura desψ ka. Zenbu de Hyaku-go-
jū-man'en hodo desψ.

UNIT TWO

FLUENCY PRACTICE 11: 1 Do you understand? Yes, I
understand. 2 Are you going home? Yes, I'm going home after
this. 3 I, etc. will do my best. 4 Are you working the day after
tomorrow? 5 Are you (literally 'a person') from the export
section? No, I'm not. 6 Machimasψ ka. Hai, machimasψ.
7 Ashita ikimasψ ka. 8 Raishū aimasψ. 9 Isogimasψ ka.
10 Katō-san desψ ka. Iie, chigaimasψ.

FLUENCY PRACTICE 12: 1 I, etc. play sport. 2 I, etc. read a newspaper. 3 The consultant writes a report. 4 She makes a phone call. 5 Do you, etc. smoke? 6 Watashi wa tegami o kakimasい. 7 Watashi-tachi wa terebi o mimasい. 8 Watashi wa shashin o torimasい. 9 Repōto o kakimasい ka. 10 Denwa o kakemasい ka.

FLUENCY PRACTICE 13: 1 I, etc. am going back to the U.K. tomorrow. 2 I, etc. am going to Mr Tanaka's office. 3 Does this train go to Otemachi? 4 I, etc. am going on a business trip to Nagoya. 5 Mr Suzuki is coming here. 6 Kono densha wa Shibuya ni ikimasい ka. 7 Hoteru ni kaerimasい ka. 8 Watashi ni denwa o kakemasい ka. 9 Mochizuki-san wa kore kara kimasい. 10 Kaigi ni demasい ka.

FLUENCY PRACTICE 14: 1 The accountant explained the problem. 2 Did you collect the information? 3 Did you have (literally 'eat') lunch? 4 Did Mr Tanaka see the catalogue? 5 Did you read the consultant's report? 6 Konsarutanto wa repōto o kakimashita. 7 Shinbun o kaimashita ka. 8 Mutō-san ni fakkいsu o okurimashita ka. 9 Dētabēsu o tsukaimashita ka. 10 Hisho wa denwa o kakemashita ka.

FLUENCY PRACTICE 15: 1 I, etc. do not understand. 2 Won't you see a film? 3 Won't you eat some o-konomi-yaki? 4 Won't you drink some rice wine? 5 Aren't you going back to Kobe tomorrow? 6 Machimasen ka. 7 Tabemasen ka. 8 Gorufu o yarimasen ka. 9 Bīru o nomimasen ka. 10 O-sushi o tabemasen ka.

FLUENCY PRACTICE 16: 1 Did you play golf? No, I didn't. 2 Mr Okazaki did not agree. 3 I, etc. did not hear Mr Ohta's speech. 4 We did not meet the department head. 5 Didn't you send the fax to Mr Clarke? 6 Kare wa dētabēsu o tsukaimasen deshita. 7 Konsarutanto wa repōto o yomimasen deshita. 8 Okいsan wa eiga o mimasen deshita ka. 9 Bengo-shi wa Sいmisu-san ni mondai o setsumei shimasen deshita ka. 10 Kaikei-shi wa kaigi ni demasen deshita.

FLUENCY PRACTICE 17: 1 Let's begin. 2 Shall we drink some rice wine? 3 Let's do our best. 4 Shall we go to the bank? 5 In that case, let's meet next month. 6 Yasumimashō. 7 Hairimashō ka. 8 Kono hon o yomimashō ka. 9 Yamemashō ka. 10 Sore de wa, raigetsu gorufu o yarimashō ka.

FLUENCY PRACTICE 18: 1 What time is it (now)? It's three o'clock.   2 What time is it? It's eleven o'clock.   3 It's four o'clock.   4 It's ten past seven.   5 It's twenty-five past twelve.   6 Nan-ji desψ ka. Roku-ji desψ.   7 Ima nan-ji desψ ka. Yoji-han desψ.   8 Jū-ichi-ji jū-go-fun desψ.   9 Kuji jū-go-fun-mae desψ.   10 Shichiji ni-jū-go-fun desψ.

FLUENCY PRACTICE 19: 1 The meeting is until half past three.   2 The conference starts (literally 'from') tomorrow.   3 The train goes from Shinjuku station.   4 I, etc. go from Tokyo to Osaka.   5 It's from nine o'clock until five o'clock.   6 Kare wa ashita made hatarakimasψ.   7 Watashi wa Akasaka made ikimasψ.   8 Kōgi wa hachi-ji made desψ.   9 Watashi wa Narita Kūkō kara hoteru ni ikimasψ.   10 Kaigi wa ni-ji kara go-ji made desψ.

FLUENCY PRACTICE 20: 1 Please give me some coffee.   2 Please give me that pen.   3 Please give me some orange juice.   4 Please give me a 100 Yen piece.   5 Please give me that cake.   6 Bīru o kudasai. Bīru (o) o-negai shimasψ.   7 Sono/Ano hon o kudasai. Sono/Ano hon (o) o-negai shimasψ.   8 Kagi o kudasai.   9 Chiketto o kudasai.   10 Panfuretto o kudasai.

UNIT THREE

FLUENCY PRACTICE 21: 1 There is a problem.   2 Have you got money? Yes, I have a little.   3 I have an appointment.   4 Have you got paper? Yes, I have.   5 I, etc. have a personal computer.   6 Chiketto/Kippu ga arimasψ.   7 O-jikan wa arimasψ ka. Hai, arimasψ.   8 Inkan ga mittsu arimasψ.   9 Kψrejitto kādo wa arimasψ ka. Hai, yon-mai arimasψ.   10 Ginkō ga arimasψ.

FLUENCY PRACTICE 22: 1 There is an engineer.   2 There are mosquitoes. 3 Mr Suzuki is here/there.   4 Is the department head in/there? Yes, he is.   5 Is Mr Nakajima from Chiyoda Printing there? Yes, he is.   6 Eki-in ga imasψ.   7 Annai-gakari wa imasψ ka. Hai, imasψ.   8 Asano-san ga imasψ.   9 Konsarutanto wa imasψ ka. Hai, imasψ.   10 Jōnzu Asoshiētsu no Jonzū-san ga imasψ.

FLUENCY PRACTICE 23: 1 There is a fax machine at the station.   2 There is a lawyer in the room.   3 There is a phone in the corridor.   4 Mr White from the U.S.A. is in the entrance hall.   5 There is a petrol station over there.   6 Jimu-sho ni konpyūtā

ga arimasψ.   7 Saifu ni o-kane ga arimasψ.   8 Jimu-sho ni konsarutanto ga imasψ.   9 Nimotsu ni pasψpōto ga arimasψ.
10 Hon'ya ni chizu wa arimasψ ka.

FLUENCY PRACTICE 24: 1 There are no word processors in the hotel.   2 I'm sorry, but there's no suki-yaki.   3 Isn't Mr Tsuji in/there?   4 There is nothing in the drawer.   5 Isn't there anybody in/there?   6 Jikan ga arimasen.   7 Yoshizawa-san wa imasen.   8 Sumimasen ga, chiketto/kippu ga arimasen.
9 Heya ni wa nanimo arimasen.   10 Kaigi-shitsu ni wa daremo imasen.

FLUENCY PRACTICE 25: 1 I, etc. am writing a fax (message) in English.   2 Let's go to Narita Airport by Limousine Bus.
3 I, etc. paid the bill in Japanese Yen.   4 Mr Smith, the company president, went back by plane.   5 I, etc. spoke on the phone in Japanese.   6 Watashi wa wāpψro de repōto o kakimashɨta.   7 Watashi wa Shinkansen de Ōsaka ni/e ikimasψ.
8 Chika-tetsu de ikimashō.   9 Kare wa Nihon-go de sψpīchi o shimashīta.   10 Watashi wa takψshī de hoteru ni/e kaerimasψ.

FLUENCY PRACTICE 26: 1 I read a book on the plane.
2 They, etc. held a conference in Kobe.   3 The reporter wrote an article in the library.   4 Let's meet in the entrance hall of the company.   5 Let's take a photo of the machines at the factory.
6 Watashi wa kūkō de asa-gohan o tabemashɨta.   7 Sono/Ano kissa-ten de hanashimashō.   8 Watashi wa ginkō de o-kane o kaemashɨta.   9 Yoyogi eki de aimashō.   10 Hoteru no heya de terebi o mimashō.

FLUENCY PRACTICE 27: 1 What time do you go to bed? I go to bed at eleven o'clock.   2 What day is it today? It's Wednesday.
3 Let's meet at six o'clock in the lobby at the company.   4 I, etc. arrived at Haneda Airport at ten to seven.   5 When does the conference end? It ends at five o'clock.   6 Mītingu wa itsu hajimarimasψ ka. Jū-ji jū-go-fun ni hajimarimasψ.   7 Itsu owarimasψ ka. Jū-ji yon-jū-go-fun ni owarimasψ.   8 Torēdo fea wa itsu hajimarimasψ ka. Ka-yōbi ni hajimarimasψ.   9 Nan-ji ni tsukimasψ ka. Go-ji juppun-mae ni tsukimasψ.   10 Kachō wa yoji-han ni mītingu ni demashɨta.

FLUENCY PRACTICE 29: 1 Excuse me, but are you Miss Pritchard from the U.K.?   2 Mr Okazaki (who is a teacher) said so.   3 Where did you study Japanese?   4 Mr Takeuchi from

Yokohama Machinery is here/there. 5 Won't you eat some suki-yaki or something? 6 O-kyakɯ-sama ga irasshaimasɯ ka. 7 Fuku-buchō wa kaigi-shitsu ni irasshaimasɯ. 8 Makuhari Messe ni/e irasshaimasɯ ka. 9 Shachō-sama wa irasshaimasɯ ka. 10 Terebi o goran ni narimasen ka.

FLUENCY PRACTICE 30: 1 The toilet is over there. 2 In that case, I'll come tomorrow. 3 The conference room is [on] the second floor. 4 There are some chairs over there. Please sit down. 5 I, etc. am going on a business trip to Hakata. 6 Watakɯshi wa Jōnzu to mōshimasɯ. 7 Watakɯshi wa ashɨta Ōsaka ni/e mairimasɯ. 8 Achira/Asoko ni denwa ga gozaimasɯ. 9 Shachō wa kyonen Nihon ni/e mairimashɨta. 10 Okazaki-san no repōto o haiken shimashɨta.

UNIT FOUR

FLUENCY PRACTICE 31: 1 I, etc. went to Asakusa and bought some souvenirs. 2 I, etc. went to Yokohama and met Mr Suzuki from Nissan. 3 I am going to Shizuoka tomorrow and coming back the day after. 4 I, etc. went into the entrance hall and made a telephone call. 5 I, etc. got on the underground and went back to my hotel. 6 Watashi wa mise ni/e itte, terehon kādo o kaimashɨta. 7 Watashi wa kitte o katte, e-hagaki o okurimashɨta. 8 Watashi wa denwa o kakete, hoteru no yoyaku o kakunin shimashɨta. 9 Watashi wa dētabēsu o tsukatte, shiryō o atsumemashɨta. 10 Watashi wa pasɯpōto o nakɯshɨte, Igirisu Taishi-kan ni ikimashɨta.

FLUENCY PRACTICE 32: 1 She is doing her best. 2 He is making a phone call now. 3 Mr Itoh, the department head, is doing some dealings in Tokyo. 4 Excuse me, but I'm looking for Royal Furniture's English annual report. 5 I, etc. am living in London now. 6 Saitō-san wa shinbun o yonde imasɯ. 7 Kanojo wa kyō, repōto o kaite imasɯ. 8 Andō-san wa Kōbe no kōjō de hataraite imasɯ. 9 Kachō wa ima, ohiru o tabete imasɯ. 10 Shinbun kisha wa kiji o kaite imashɨta.

FLUENCY PRACTICE 33: 1 I, etc. am really tired. 2 The door is open. 3 The section head has gone out. 4 The train hasn't come yet. 5 Is he married? 6 Kekkon shɨte imasɯ ka. Iie, mada dokɯshin desɯ. 7 Kono mado wa shimatte imasɯ. 8 Denki ga kiete imasɯ. 9 Kono michi wa konde imasɯ. 10 Kabin ga kowarete imasɯ.

FLUENCY PRACTICE 34: 1 Please phone me the day after tomorrow. 2 Please send a fax to Mr Yoshioka. 3 Please wait a moment. 4 Won't you translate this into English? 5 Please listen carefully (literally 'well') to the company president's explanation. 6 Eigo de hanashite kudasai. 7 Shashin o totte kudasaimasen ka. 8 Keiyaku o yoku yonde kudasai. 9 Shōsai o fakkஶsu de okutte kudasai. 10 Kono kozutsumi o honbu e/ni okutte kudasai.

FLUENCY PRACTICE 35: 1 After I, etc. go back to the U.K., I will definitely write you letters. 2 After I, etc. graduated, I went to Japan. 3 After I, etc. had had dinner, I went to a bar. 4 After I, etc. have seen the plan, I will discuss it with Mr Yoshida. 5 After I, etc. looked up the train on the timetable, I bought the ticket. 6 Kare wa kōhī o nonde kara, shinbun o yomimashita. 7 Watashi wa kaisha no anyuaru repōto o yonde kara, kabu o kaimashita. 8 Kanojo wa fakkஶsu o okutte kara, (uchi e/ni) kaerimashita. 9 Watashi-tachi wa Nagoya ni tsuite kara, hoteru o sagashimashita. 10 Watashi wa asa-gohan o tabete kara, dekakemashita.

FLUENCY PRACTICE 36: 1 Before I, etc. used the computer, first I read the manual. 2 Before I, etc. meet Mr Himeno, I'm going to the bank. 3 Before I, etc. attended the conference, I made a phone call. 4 Before you go back to the U.K., please confirm your flight (literally 'plane'). 5 Before we, etc. use the credit card, let's check the exchange rate. 6 Watashi-tachi wa Nihon e/ni iku mae ni, Nihon'en o kaimashita. 7 Iku mae ni, o-kanjō o haratte kudasai. 8 Watashi wa shachō ni au mae ni, anyuara repōto o yomimashita. 9 Nihon e/ni iku mae ni, hoteru no yoyaku o kakunin shite kudasai. 10 Watashi ga Igirisu e/ni kaeru mae ni, ippai nomi ni ikimashō.

FLUENCY PRACTICE 37: 1 I, etc. was tired, so I rested straight away. 2 My work is (literally 'has') finished, so I'll (take the liberty of) leave(ing) before you. 3 It doesn't matter what, so try saying (something). 4 I, etc. am in a hurry, so please hand the report in. 5 I've drunk rice wine, so I won't drive the car. 6 Watashi wa bejitarian desஶ kara, o-niku wa tabemasen. 7 Watashi wa kesa Nihon ni tsuita bakari desஶ kara, totemo tsukarete imasஶ. 8 Kare wa Nihon-go ga wakarimasen kara, Eigo de hanashimashō. 9 Watashi-tachi wa jikan ga arimasஶ kara, kissa-ten ni haitte ocha de mo nomimashō. 10 Shachō wa ima orimasen kara, chotto o-machi kudasai.

FLUENCY PRACTICE 38: 1 Can I, etc. buy a ticket here? 2 Can you, etc. confirm the details by Thursday next week? 3 There is a problem with the voltage, so you can't use this machine in Japan. 4 The accountant can't answer that question. 5 Mr Katō's secretary can't use a word processor. 6 Gorufu wa dekimasɯ ka. 7 Bengo-shi wa sono mondai o setsumei dekimasɯ. 8 Yūbin-kyoku kara fakkɯsu o okuru koto ga dekimasɯ ka. 9 Chokɯsetsu Nagoya e/ni iku koto ga dekimasɯ ka./Nagoya e/ni chokɯsetsu iku koto ga dekimasɯ ka. 10 Kanai wa byōki deshɨta kara, pātī e/ni iku koto ga dekimasen deshɨta.

FLUENCY PRACTICE 39: 1 I, etc. (have) had breakfast. 2 I, etc. went to London last year. 3 I, etc. saw an interesting programme on television last night. 4 They (have) bought a new computer. 5 Have you read this book? 6 Bengo-shi wa keiyaku o yonda. 7 Watashi wa kazoku no tame ni pɯrezento o katta. 8 Watashi wa ototoi Nihon ni tsuita. 9 Kudamono o katta? 10 Senshū Yamaguchi-san ni atta?

UNIT FIVE

FLUENCY PRACTICE 40: 1 It's black. 2 I'm happy. 3 This flower is red. 4 Are you embarrassed? 5 That person is awful. 6 Shiroi desɯ. 7 Kono hon wa kiiroi desɯ. 8 Sono hana wa aoi desɯ ka. 9 Totemo tanoshii desɯ. 10 Ima o-isogashii desɯ ka.

FLUENCY PRACTICE 41: 1 It's a good idea. 2 She is an interesting person. 3 Is it a big company? No, it's a small company. 4 That is an old company. 5 Isn't there a more interesting film? 6 Sore wa atarashii biru desɯ. 7 Sore wa akai jidō-sha/kuruma desɯ ka. 8 Sore wa hontō ni omoshiroi hanashi desɯ. 9 Kare wa warui hɨto de wa arimasen. 10 Kanojo wa kibishii sensei de wa arimasen.

FLUENCY PRACTICE 42: 1 It's got very warm. 2 The plane arrived late. 3 That company's shares have gone up (literally, 'got higher') recently. 4 I, etc. can understand Japanese well, but I can't speak it. (Note: **wa** is used, rather than **ga** to imply the contrast with being able to understand Japanese.) 5 The price of that product has got cheaper because of (literally, 'in') the recession. 6 Watashi-tachi wa osoku tsukimashɨta. 7 Kuraku narimashɨta. 8 Totemo atsuku narimashɨta. 9 Watashi wa sono hɨto o yoku shitte imasɯ. 10 Kaneko-san wa tokei o yasɯku kaimashɨta.

FLUENCY PRACTICE 43: 1 Was Mr Suzuki's presentation interesting? 2 Hakata Electric's shares were cheap. 3 I was busy. 4 That hotel was good. 5 The party was very enjoyable. 6 Watashi wa hazukashɨkatta desѱ. 7 Kinō wā suzushɨkatta desѱ. 8 Sono hon'yaku wa takakatta desѱ ka. 9 Ano shōhin wa totemo yasѱkatta desѱ. 10 Kyonen no Nihon no natsu wa mushi-atsukatta desѱ.

FLUENCY PRACTICE 44: 1 Are you envious? No, I'm not envious. 2 Is Japanese grammar difficult? No, it's not so difficult. 3 Is that joke funny? No, it's not at all funny. 4 This food (literally, 'cookery') is not very tasty. 5 That product is not expensive. 6 Yasѱku arimasen/nai desѱ. 7 Atsui desѱ ka. Iie, atsuku arimasen. Suzushii desѱ. 8 Takai desѱ ka. Iie, zenzen takaku arimasen/nai desѱ. 9 Kanji wa muzukashii desѱ ka. Iie, zenzen muzukashɨku arimasen/nai desѱ. 10 Sono hanashi wa omoshiroi desѱ ka. Iie, amari omoshiroku arimasen/nai desѱ.

FLUENCY PRACTICE 45: 1 It wasn't very difficult. 2 I, etc. wasn't at all busy. 3 The food in that restaurant wasn't very good. 4 I, etc. bought a personal computer yesterday, but it wasn't cheap. 5 Mr Suzuki's speech wasn't very interesting. 6 Pѱrezento wa sonna ni takaku arimasen deshɨta/nakatta desѱ. 7 Shiken wa zenzen yasashɨku arimasen deshɨta/nakatta desѱ. 8 Kaigi wa amari omoshiroku arimasen deshɨta/nakatta desѱ. 9 Konsarutanto no happyō wa zenzen omoshiroku arimasen deshɨta/nakatta desѱ. 10 Pātī wa tanoshɨkatta desѱ ka. Iie, zenzen tanoshɨku arimasen deshɨta/nakatta desѱ.

FLUENCY PRACTICE 46: 1 The apple was hard and sour. 2 It was difficult and I, etc. gave up. 3 I, etc. was busy and I didn't go to the conference. 4 This flat is good and spacious, isn't it? (Note that ii comes second in Japanese.) 5 It was hot and I, etc. couldn't study. 6 Kono bīru wa tsumetakѱte oishii desѱ. 7 Heya wa semakѱte, kitanakatta desѱ. 8 Igirisu no fuyu wa nagukѱte samui desѱ. 9 Sono mise no ryōri wa aburappokѱte mazui desѱ. 10 Sono kissa-ten wa takakѱte, oishɨku arimasen.

FLUENCY PRACTICE 47: 1 I, etc. don't understand. 2 Won't you come with me (literally, 'go together')? 3 I'll have this one, not that one. (Literally, 'It isn't that one and I'll decide on this one.') 4 He, etc. can't speak Japanese at all. 5 It was a nuisance not having a dictionary. (Literally, 'There wasn't a dictionary and it was a nuisance.') 6 Kore wa ichi-man'en-satsu de wa nai. 7 Ippai

nomanai?   8 Nihon no terebi o minai?   9 Kare wa kaikei-shi
de wa nakɰte, bengo-shi desɰ.   10 Boku wa ii hoteru ni
tomaranakatta.

FLUENCY PRACTICE 48: 1 I want to walk to the Ginza. (**Ne** adds
a friendly tone, here.)   2 Yesterday, I, etc. wanted to go to a trade
fair in Tokyo.   3 I, etc. wanted to buy some Japanese souvenirs.
4 I, etc. did not want to be a nuisance to Mr Kawaguchi.   5 Mr
Tanaka did not want to speak about it (literally, 'that thing').
6 Sushi ga/o tabetai desɰ.   7 Igirisu ni/e fakkɰsu o okuritai desɰ.
8 Sono eiga o mitai desɰ.   9 Nihon ni ikitai desɰ.   10 Nihon-go
o benkyō shitai desɰ./Nihon-go no benkyō o shitai desɰ.

FLUENCY PRACTICE 49: 1 I, etc. probably won't go to the
Osaka branch. (The **wa** implies that he will go to one of the other
branches.)   2 The reporter is probably writing an article.
3 Would you like some Japanese tea?   4 Mr Tanaka has
probably already arrived in Japan.   5 Russian is probably more
difficult than English.   6 Tabun ashɨta yuki ga furu deshō./Ashɨta
tabun yuki ga furu deshō.   7 Nihon-go wa totemo muzukashii
deshō.   8 Kawasaki-san ni aitaku nai deshō.   9 Hoteru wa
takakatta deshō.   10 Mō repōto o dashimashɨta kara, tabun
daijōbu deshō.

UNIT SIX

FLUENCY PRACTICE 50: 1 Are you well? I'm fine, thank you.
2 Sorry, but that is impossible.   3 That hotel is quiet, but that
hotel over there is noisy.   4 A new computer became
necessary./I, etc. came to need a new computer.   5 The
underground in Japan is convenient and cheap.   6 Kanai wa
byōki desɰ.   7 Kono zasshi wa hitsuyō desɰ.   8 Kono shōhin
wa totemo benri desɰ.   9 Kare wa kokɰsai-teki ni yūmei na
kenchiku-ka desɰ.   10 Kare wa shōjiki de, shinrai dekimasɰ.

FLUENCY PRACTICE 51: 1 That (place over there) is a beautiful
garden, isn't it?   2 It's not a very beautiful building.   3 London is
not a quiet city.   4 I, etc. did something stupid.   5 I, etc. (have)
forgot(ten) something important (literally 'an important thing').
6 Sore wa ōki na kaisha desɰ.   7 Kore wa totemo benri na
shōhin desɰ.   8 Sore/Are wa iya na keiken deshɨta.   9 Shibuya
wa nigiyaka na machi desɰ.   10 Suzuki-san no okɰsan wa yūmei
na joyū desɰ.

FLUENCY PRACTICE 52: 1 It wasn't necessary. 2 These figures are not accurate. 3 That consultant is not very famous. 4 I can speak a little Japanese, but I'm not good at it. (Note that although the object of **dekiru** ('can [speak]') is usually indicated by **ga** (not **o**), **ga** is replaced by **wa** here as there is an idea of contrast.) 5 The location of the hotel in Nagoya wasn't very convenient. 6 Sore wa tekitō de wa arimasen. 7 Shiken wa amari kantan de wa arimasen deshita/de wa nakatta desu. 8 Manyuaru wa fukuzatsu de wa arimasen/de wa nai desu. 9 Kōen wa amari shizuka de wa arimasen deshita. 10 Sore wa amari taisetsu de wa arimasen deshita/de wa nakatta desu.

FLUENCY PRACTICE 53: 1 I am weak at Japanese (and) ... (Modest remarks are often left unfinished.) 2 Do you like yaki-tori? 3 He likes swimming and I like jogging. 4 They are good at Japanese, but I'm not good at it. 5 There are many people in Tokyo. 6 (Nihon no) o-kashi wa o-suki desu ka. 7 Sore wa hoshiku arimasen/nai desu. 8 Atama/ha/onaka ga itai desu. 9 Nihon-go wa jōzu de wa arimasen. 10 Musume wa nattō ga kirai desu.

FLUENCY PRACTICE 54: 1 Would it be all right for me, etc. to speak to the head of the export section? 2 Would it be all right for me, etc. to see the company president? 3 Is it all right for me, etc. to speak about the conference? 4 Is it all right for me, etc. to make a phone call? 5 Would it be all right for me, etc. to rest here a while? 6 Shashin o totte mo ii desu ka. 7 Tabako o sutte mo ii desu ka. 8 Sono/Ano shinbun o yonde mo ii desu ka. 9 Mado o akete mo ii desu ka. 10 Eigo de hanashite mo ii desu ka.

FLUENCY PRACTICE 55: 1 Please don't smoke. 2 Please don't take photos here. 3 Please don't hold back. (Although **enryo** is a virtue, one may well be asked not to be too virtuous!) 4 Please don't say anything before the presentation next week. 5 Please don't phone before six o'clock. 6 Kore o tsukawanaide kudasai. 7 Sono/Ano botan o osanaide kudasai. 8 Ie no naka de kutsu o hakanaide kudasai. 9 Takushī de ikanaide kudasai. 10 Ōki na koe de hanasanaide kudasai.

FLUENCY PRACTICE 56: 1 You mustn't tell anybody (literally, 'a person') from another company. 2 You mustn't go home before a superior. 3 You mustn't work in Japan without a visa. 4 You mustn't blow your nose in a public place. 5 This is a library, so

you mustn't speak in a loud voice.   6 Hakubutsu-kan no naka de
wa shashin o totte wa ikemasen.   7 Soko ni kuruma o tomete wa
ikemasen.   8 Soko de matte ite wa ikemasen.   9 Neru mae ni,
kōhī o nonde wa ikemasen.   10 Mītingu no toki ni Eigo de
hanashite wa ikemasen.

FLUENCY PRACTICE 57: 1 Did you go (then)?   2 I, etc. want to
buy a word processor ...   3 I want to know about Osaka
Chemicals in detail.   4 I don't know how to use the computer ...
5 You're good at Japanese. How long have you been studying?
I've studied for about four months.   6 Kaeru n desψ ka.
7 Watashi wa heya o yoyaku shitai n desψ.   8 Watashi wa
Kurita-san ni aitai n desψ.   9 Dō shita n desψ ka. Atama ga itai n
desψ.   10 Gorufu ga o-jōzu desu ne. Dono kurai yatte irassharψ
n desψ ka. Yonen gurai yatte orimasψ. (Note the use of **-te
irassharu** and **-te oru** which are the Honorific and Humble
equivalents respectively of **-te iru**.)

UNIT SEVEN

FLUENCY PRACTICE 58: 1 I, etc. have seen Mount Fuji.   2 I,
etc. have drunk Japanese rice wine.   3 Have you (ever) read that
book?   4 Have you ever been abroad?   5 Have you ever
experienced an earthquake?   6 Watashi wa kaigi de sψpīchi o
shita koto ga arimasψ.   7 Sono/Ano eiga o mita koto ga arimasψ
ka.   8 Kyōto ni/e itta koto ga arimasψ ka.   9 Doitsu de Nihon-go
o benkyō shita koto ga arimasψ ka./Doitsu de Nihon-go no benkyō
o shita koto ga arimasψ ka.   10 Sushi/O-sushi o tabeta koto ga
arimasψ ka.

FLUENCY PRACTICE 59: 1 Let's begin.   2 Let's go to bed
early.   3 Well, shall we go straight away?   4 Let's go in there
and have a meal.   5 Let's try asking that woman.   6 Owari ni
shiyō.   7 Akirameyō ka./Yameyō ka.   8 Sorosoro kaerō.
9 Ippai nomō.   10 Hoteru no resepψshon/uketsuke de sore o
kakunin shiyō.

FLUENCY PRACTICE 60: 1 He said that he would come.
2 I, etc. (think that I) would like to go to Japan.   3 I, etc. think
that that person is the company president.   4 I think that politics
is interesting.   5 Do you think that R&D is important?
6 Watashi wa sono hoteru ga ii to omoimasψ.   7 Watashi wa
sono resψtoran wa takai to omoimasψ.   8 Suzuki-san wa sono
resψtoran wa yoku nai to itte imasψ./Suzuki-san wa sono resψtoran

wa yoku nai to iimasɰ. (**Iimasɰ** implies that he often says this; **itte imasɰ** implies that he said it a moment ago.) 9 Watashi wa mondai ga takɰsan aru to omoimashɨta. 10 Kare wa Nihon-go ga muzukashii to iimashɨta.

FLUENCY PRACTICE 61: 1 Who is the person who made the presentation? 2 I, etc. don't have much chance to speak Japanese. 3 It's about the matter we talked about on the phone ... (**O-hanashi suru** is the Humble form of **hanasu**, 'speak'.) 4 There are no companies where they use such old machines. 5 I bumped into a teacher who is researching economics in Japan at a party. 6 Watashi wa kinō kaita tegami o dashimashɨta. 7 Asoko ni tatte iru otoko no hɨto wa dare desɰ ka. 8 Nakamura-san ga shōkai shɨta josei no kata wa dare desɰ ka. 9 Watashi ga ototoi deta kaigi wa amari omoshiroku arimasen deshɨta/nakatta desɰ. 10 Kare-ra ga kaigi de hanashɨta koto wa kankyō mondai deshɨta.

FLUENCY PRACTICE 62: 1 My friend gave me this ticket. (**Ga** is used as the sentence is probably a reply to 'Who gave you that ticket?' and **tomodachi** is new information.) 2 I, etc. gave the information I had collected to the consultant. 3 I, etc. received this fax from Yoyogi Industrial. 4 Please give this present to your wife. 5 This is the novel I received [Hum.] from Mr Shimizu. 6 Watashi wa Saitō-san ni meishi o agemashɨta. 7 (Watashi no) tomodachi wa (watashi ni) kono shashin o kuremashɨta. (It would not be good Japanese to use **watashi** twice in this sentence.) 8 Watashi wa Kudō-san kara/ni kono techō o moraimashɨta. 9 Watashi wa Tsuji-san kara/ni denwa o moraimashɨta. 10 Okɰsan ga kureta o-kashi/kēki wa hontō ni oishɨkatta desɰ.

FLUENCY PRACTICE 63: 1 It's best to go now. 2 It would be better to speak Japanese. 3 It's best not to buy clothing in Japan, as it's expensive. 4 You, etc. had better talk about that with the department head. 5 It's best to learn Japanese, as Japan has become a great economic country. 6 Denwa o kaketa hō ga ii desɰ (yo)./Denwa shɨta hō ga ii desɰ (yo). 7 Takɰshī de ikanai hō ga ii desɰ (yo). 8 Hoteru o yoyaku shɨta hō ga ii desɰ (yo). 9 Fakkɰsu o okutta hō ga hayai desɰ (yo). 10 Dētabēsu de kakunin shɨta hō ga ii desɰ (yo).

FLUENCY PRACTICE 64: 1 Tomorrow may be busy, too. 2 I, etc. may write the report on the word processor. 3 It may have been all right. 4 The section head may be angry because of that.

5 The director may have gone to the conference.   6 Kare wa kaikei-shi ka mo shiremasen.   7 Watashi wa asatte Kōbe ni/e iku ka mo shiremasen.   8 Sono kaisha no kabu wa takai ka mo shiremasen.   9 Kaigi wa kyanseru sareru ka mo shiremasen.   10 Ashita ame (ga furu) ka mo shiremasen.

UNIT EIGHT

FLUENCY PRACTICE 65: 1 If you understand how the machine works, please tell me.   2 If only we, etc. have time, we intend to go to Kamakura or somewhere.   3 If you're a man, you say 'kana', not 'kashira'.   4 I wonder if it will be quicker and cheaper to go by train than [to take] a taxi.   5 If you need it immediately, please come and get it in ten minutes time.   6 Yasɰkereba, kaimasɰ.   7 Kono botan o oseba, kikai ga ugokimasɰ. 8 Fakkɰsu o okureba, tsugi no hi ni henji ga kuru ka mo shiremasen.   9 Hitsuyō nara, repōto o agemasɰ/sashi-agemasɰ. 10 Motto renshū sureba, kanji ga jōzu ni narimasɰ.

FLUENCY PRACTICE 66: 1 I, etc. must do my best.   2 Both of us, etc. must make an effort.   3 It's a pity, but I think I must give up.   4 If we, etc. don't hurry, we will miss the train.   5 We, etc. may have to wait a little longer.   6 Watashi-tachi wa ima, ikanakereba narimasen.   7 Nihon-go de hanasanakereba narimasen.   8 Nedan ga takaku nakereba, watashi ga kaimasɰ. 9 Watashi wa kin-yōbi made ni repōto o kakanakereba narimasen.   10 Watashi wa ashita, hatarakanakereba naranai ka mo shiremasen.

FLUENCY PRACTICE 67: 1 I, etc. will contact Mr Clarke after I've returned to Britain.   2 Once I, etc. had tried doing it, it wasn't as difficult as I'd thought.   3 If it's all right by you, I'll do it instead. (The **ga** implies 'rather than anyone else'.)   4 Would you tell Mr Tamura, after the preparations have been made? 5 If I don't get through, I'll try (literally, 'phone') again later. 6 Nihon ni tsuitara, denwa o kakete kudasai./Nihon ni tsuitara, denwa shite kudasai./Nihon ni tsuitara, denwa o kudasai. 7 Shigoto ga owattara, ippai nomimasen ka.   8 Watashi wa sotsugyō shitara, Kanazawa Shōji ni hairimasɰ.   9 Yamada-san ni attara, watashi no meishi o watashite kudasai.   10 Maniattara, shichiji jū-nana-fun no densha ni norimashō.

FLUENCY PRACTICE 68: 1 When you turn right, you will be able to see the traffic lights.   2 I don't think you can do it if you don't have permission. 3 I think your Japanese will get better when you go to Japan. 4 If you read this report, you'll understand the causes of that accident. 5 If you don't make your preparations on the early side, you'll be late. 6 Michi o wataru to, byōin ga miemasɰ. 7 Kaisu-ken o kau to, motto yasɰkute benri desɰ. 8 Eki no de-guchi ni tsuku to, hidari-gawa ni kōshū denwa ga arimasɰ. 9 Manyuaru no san-juppēji/san-jippēji o yomu to wakarimasɰ. 10 Hikō-ki de iku to, jū-ni-jikan gurai kakaru to omoimasɰ.

FLUENCY PRACTICE 69: 1 Can you drink rice wine? 2 Can you use chopsticks? (Using **o** rather than **wa** in this sentence implies that the speaker presumes you can.) 3 Can you make a phone call in Japanese? 4 Can I pay by credit card? 5 I, etc. can write hiragana and katakana, but I can't write kanji. 6 Oyogemasɰ ka. 7 Nihon-go wa yomemasɰ ka. 8 O-sushi wa taberaremasɰ ka. 9 Ashɨta no pātɨ ni/e ikemasɰ ka. 10 Nihon de jidō-sha o unten dekimasɰ ka./Nihon de jidō-sha no unten ga dekimasɰ ka.

FLUENCY PRACTICE 70: 1 I, etc. was watching television as I listened to the music. 2 She studied her kanji (literally 'while she rode') on the train. 3 I, etc. was using the computer as I was speaking on the telephone. 4 I was speaking Japanese whilst thinking in English, so I ended up saying something stupid. 5 I, etc. was reading a Japanese patent using a dictionary. 6 Watashi wa terebi o minagara, tegami o kakimasɰ. 7 Watashi wa wisɰkī o nominagara, buchō to hanashɨte imashɨta. 8 Konsarutanto wa chōsa o shinagara, repōto o kaite imashɨta. 9 Shokuji o shinagara, hanashimasen ka. 10 Watashi-tachi wa chizu o minagara ikimashɨta kara, zuibun jikan ga kakarimashɨta.

FLUENCY PRACTICE 71: 1 I am called Eric Jones. 2 There is somebody called Mr, etc. Murakami. 3 I, etc. wrote a report entitled (literally, 'called') 'Environmental problems'. 4 What does **bin** mean? It means 'bottle'. 5 How do you say **kekkyoku** in English? It's 'eventually'. 6 Watashi wa Sērā Howaito to iimasɰ./Watakɰshi wa Sērā Howaito to mōshimasɰ. 7 Kono kanji wa dō yuu imi desɰ ka. 8 Watashi wa Tanaka to yuu seiji-ka ni aimashɨta. 9 Kabin no 'ka' wa dō yuu imi desɰ ka. Hana to yuu imi desɰ. 10 'Environmental problem' wa Nihon-go de nan to iimasɰ ka./Nihon-go de 'environmental problem' wa nan to iimasɰ ka. 'Kankyō mondai' to iimasɰ.

FLUENCY PRACTICE 72: 1 I hear that there will be such a plan in the future. 2 I hear that they can do the work by Thursday. 3 I hear that he/she is writing a book about Japanese databases. 4 I hear that he/she is having an argument with Mr, etc. Yoshida. 5 I hear that Mr, etc. Mochizuki and Mr, etc. Yamamoto do not get on very well. 6 Sono shiken wa amari muzukashiku nai sō desⱳ. 7 Shōhin no shitsu ga amari yoku nai sō desⱳ. 8 Konsarutanto wa dare desⱳ ka. Bēkā Asoshiētsu no Bēkā-san da sō desⱳ. 9 Kare wa Eigo ga yoku dekiru/hanaseru sō desⱳ. 10 Kanojo wa Igirisu no shitsugyō mondai ni tsuite shiryō o atsumete iru sō desⱳ.

FLUENCY PRACTICE 73: 1 It looks as if the section head is busy. 2 It looks easy but in fact it's quite difficult. 3 The department head seems to be quite drunk. 4 It seems that we, etc. need to confirm the reservation (literally, 'make a confirmation of the reservation'). 5 The new product seems to be selling well. 6 Ame no yō desⱳ. 7 Shizuka na yō desⱳ. 8 Sono/Ano wāpⱳro wa kowarete iru yō desⱳ. 9 Kare-ra wa Kawaguchi-san no chōsa shiryō o tsukatte iru yō desⱳ. 10 Sono kaisha wa amari kenkyū kaihatsu o okonatte/shite/yatte inai yō desⱳ.

VOCABULARY

In the following list, the numbers refer to the Structure or Conversation in which the word first appears.

C Conversation; CV Consonant verb ending in **-eru** or **-iru**; Hon. Honorific; Hum. Humble; Pol. Polite.

a' oh 50
aburappoi oily 46
achira Pol. that (one over there); over there 30
ageru give (to an equal or superior) 30
aida: no aida ni during 63
ainiku unfortunately C12
aite other person, partner C12
akai red 37
akeru open (something) 54
akirameru give up 59
aku (something) opens 33
amai sweet 53
amari + Neg. not very 44
ame rain; **ame ga furu** to rain 49
Amerika-jin American (person) 1
annai-gakari information officer 22
annai-jo information centre/desk 23
annai panfuretto guide pamphlet C30
annai suru guide C17
ano that, those (over there) (followed by a noun) 9
ano kata Hon. he/she 6
anyuaru repōto annual report 32

aoi blue 40
apāto flat, apartment 4
are that (one) (over there) 2
arigatō thank you C10
aru there is/are; have 21; happen, be held C34
aruite iku walk 48
asa-gohan breakfast 26
asatte the day after tomorrow 11
ashita tomorrow 11
asobu play (around) 52
asoko over there 4
atama head 53
atarashii new 39
atatakai warm 42
-ate ni for (of letters, etc.) C10
atsui hot 42
atsukau deal with C36
atsumeru collect, gather (something) 14
au meet (object marked by **ni**, not **o**) 11
azukaru receive (of money) C23

bā bar 35
bāi occasion; when C12
baka da stupid 51
-ban counter for nights stayed C25

ban evening 39
ban-gohan dinner 35
bangō number 8
bangumi programme 39
basho place 52
basɯ-tei bus stop C28
bēkon bacon C6
bejitarian vegetarian 37
bengo-shi lawyer 1
benkyō suru study 29
benri da convenient 50
bentō packed lunch 6
bijinesuman businessman 3
bikkuri suru be surprised 39
bin bottle 71
biru building 41
bīru beer 15
biza visa 56
boku I, me (used by men) 47
bōrupen biro 47
botan button 37
-bu counter for pamphlets,
etc. C34
buchō department head 16
bunpō grammar 44
bɯrōshā brochure C36
byōin hospital 68
byōki da ill 50

chekku in suru check in 35
chigau differ; no 11
chiisai small 41
chijin acquaintance C34
chikai uchi ni soon C14
chikaku near (noun) C38
chika-tetsu underground
(railway) 25
chiketto ticket (for cinema,
theatre, etc.) 2
chizu map 6
chokorēto chocolate 21
chokɯsetsu directly 38

chōsa survey 70
chōsa shiryō survey
(materials) 73
chōshoku breakfast C29
Chūgoku-jin Chinese
(person) 2
chūmon order C6

da (irreg.) be 10
daiji da important 51
daitai about C20; more or
less C38
dame da no good 60
dare who? 6
daredemo everybody 50
dasu take out; post, send
(a letter); hand in 37
de is ... and C4
de gozaru Hum. be 30
de irassharu Hon. be 29
de mo or something 29
de wa in that case C6
de-au meet unintentionally,
bump into (object marked by
ni, not o) 61
de-guchi exit 68
dekakeru set out, leave 27
dekiru be able; be able to
speak 37
demo but C13
den'atsu voltage 38
denki elecricity; denki ga
tsuku a light comes on;
denki ga kieru a light goes
out 33
denki seihin electrical
products 63
densha train 13
dentō (electric) light 55
denwa telephone 2
denwa o kakeru phone 12
denwa suru phone C12

depāto department store 4
deru go/come out; attend
(object indicated by **ni**, not
o); appear 13
desɯku desk C7
dētabēsu database 14
dezainā designer 1
dō how? 45
doa door 33
dochira Pol. where? 29
Doitsu Germany 58
Doitsu-jin German (person) 1
doko where? 6
dokɯshin single (person) 33
dōmo thank you C7
donata Hon. who? 6
dono which? (followed by
noun) C38
dono kurai how long? 57
dōro road C32
dōryō colleague C12
doryoku suru make an
effort 66
do-yōbi Saturday 27
dōzo please; here you
are C10

e to 13
e-hagaki picture postcard 31
eiga film 12
Eigo English (language) 25
eigyō 3(san)-ka third sales
section C11
Eikoku Formal U.K. C36
Eikoku Kōkū British
Airways C26
eki station 4
eki-in station attendant 22
enjinia engineer 2
enpitsu pencil 3
enryo suru be restrained,
hold back 55

esa food (for animals),
feed 62

fakkɯsu fax; fax machine 8
fakkɯsu-bun fax
message 25
firumu film 53
fōku fork 4
fu-kanō da impossible 50
fu-keiki recession 42
Fuji-san Mount Fuji 58
fuku-buchō deputy
manager 29
fukumu include
(something) C37
fukutsū stomach ache C37
fumei da unclear C35
-fun minute 18
funa-bin seamail 25
Fɯransu-jin French
(person) 1
furo bath; furo-tsuki with
bath C25
furui old 41
fuyu winter 46
fuzai being out/absent C12

ga but 24
ga indicates the subject of a
sentence 21
gaijin foreigner C20
gaikoku abroad 58
gaishutsu going out C3
gaishutsu suru go out 33
ganbaru do one's best 11
gasorin sɯtando petrol
station 23
-gatsu suffix indicating the
month of the year 72
genkan entrance hall 23
genki da well, lively 50
genzai (at) present C35

getsu-yōbi Monday 27
ginkō bank 17
ginkō-ka banker 4
go five 8
go- *see following noun*
-go ni in ... time 65
gohan rice C6; meal 59
-gōkan counter for
buildings C34
goran ni naru Hon. see 29
-goro about (with times) C25
gorufu golf 12
-gōshitsu counter for room
numbers C3
gozaru Hum. exist 30
gozonji da Hon. know C22
gurai about 57
-guramu counter for
grams C24
gyōmu naiyō what a
company does C35

ha tooth 53
ha-isha dentist C38
haba-hiroku over a wide
range C36
hachi eight 8
haiken suru Hum. see;
read 30
hairu CV enter (object
indicated by **ni**) 33
haishaku suru Hum.
borrow 30
hajimaru (something)
begins 27
hajimeru begin/start
(something) 17
hajimete the first time C21
haku wear (of trousers,
footwear) 55
hakubutsu-kan museum 56
han edition 72

-han half past 18
hana flower 40
hana nose 56
hanashi story 41
hanasu speak 25
hanbai suru be on sale C34
hando meido de (Adv.)
hand-made C35
happyō presentation 43
happyō o suru make a
presentation 61
harau pay 25
hashi chopsticks 4
hataraku work 11
hayai quick; early 42
hayame ni on the early side,
early 68
hazukashii embarrassed 40
hen area, part C38
henji reply 65
henkō suru change ('to' is
ni) C15
heta da be bad at 53
heya room 8
hi day; sun; fire 39
hidari left 68
hidari-gawa left-hand
side 68
hidoi awful 40
higawari teishoku daily set
menu C5
hiki-dashi drawer 24
hikō-ki plane 2
hiku catch (of colds) 57
hiku pull; use (of dictionary,
etc.) 70
hinshitsu quality of a
product 72
hirakareru be opened (of
event) C34
hiroi wide; big (of rooms,
etc.) 40

hisho secretary 2
hito person C2
hitori-beya single room C25
hitsuyō da necessary; to
 need 50
hodo about 9
hodo (adj.) as (adj.) as 61
hoka (no) other 56
hoken insurance C37
hōmon visit C11
hon book 12
-hon counter for bottles,
 pencils, trees and other
 cylindrical things C33
honbu main branch 34
honjitsu Formal today C19
honsha main office (of
 company) C35
hontō (no) true 50
hontō ni really 33
hon'ya bookshop 23
hon'yaku suru translate 34
hoshii want (object indicated
 by **ga**, not **o**) 53
hoteru hotel 13
hyaku hundred 9
hyaku-en-dama a hundred
 Yen piece 20

ichi one 8
ichi-man'en-satsu ¥10,000
 note 47
ichi-nichi-jū all day long 52
ie house 55
ie no C4
Igirisu United Kingdom 7
Igirisu-jin British (person) 1
ii good 40
ikaga how? C4
iken opinion 63
iku go 11
ikura how much? 9

ima now 6
ima sugu immediately 65
infomēshon information C30
inkan seal 21
insatsu printing 22
inu dog 62
ippai one glass; **ippai nomu**
 have a drink 15
irasshaimase greeting used
 by shop staff et al. C5
irassharu Hon. be; go;
 come 29
iru there is/are 22
iru CV be necessary C38
iryō teate medical
 treatment C37
isogashii busy 40
isogu rush; be in a hurry 11
issho ni together 15
isu chair 30
itadaku Hum. receive 30
itai painful 53
itami pain C38
itamu be painful C38
Itaria-jin Italian (person) 2
itasu Hum. do, make 30
itsu when? 27
iya no 57
iya da unpleasant; dislike 51

ja/jā in that case C5
jānarisuto journalist 1
-ji o'clock 18
jibun (no) one's own 63
jidō-sha car 25
jikan time 21
jikkō suru execute 67
jikoku-hyō timetable 35
jimu-in clerk C34
jimu-sho office 13
jisa-boke jet-lag C27
jishin earthquake 58

jisho dictionary 35
jitsu wa in fact, actually 73
jiyū-seki free seat C9
jōdan joke 44
jogingu jogging 53
josei no kata Hon. woman 61
joyū actress 51
jōzu da good at 52
jū ten 8
jūgyō-in employee C35
junbi preparations; **junbi ga dekiru** be ready 67
jūsho address C19
jūtaku housing C36

ka mosquito 22
kaban bag 3
kabin vase 33
kabu share, stock 35
kachō section head 32
kado corner C32
kādo (credit) card C17
kaeru change (something) 26
kaeru CV return, go back; go home 11
kaette kuru come back 31
kafe café C29
kagaku chemistry 30
-kagetsu counter for months 57
kagi key 8
kagu furniture 9
-kai counter for floors 30
kaigai abroad C7
kaigi conference 13
kaigi-shitsu conference room 24
kaijō (exhibition) hall C34
kaikei-shi accountant 1
kaimono suru do the shopping 31
kaisatsu ticket barrier C32

kaisha company 5
kaisha-in company employee 6
kaisū-ken booklet of tickets 68
kakaru cost (of money); take (of time) C20
kakeru (a tooth) breaks C38
kakeru hang; **denwa o kakeru** make a phone call 12
kaku write 12
kakunin suru confirm 31
kamera camera 2
kami paper 21
kamu bite 56
Kanada-jin Canadian (person) 4
kanarazu without fail, definitely 35
kanari quite 40
kangae idea 41
kangaeru think, consider 70
kanji Chinese characters (as used in Japanese) 44
kanji feeling C13
kanjō bill 9
kankō sight-seeing C30
kankyō environment 71
kankyō mondai environmental problem 61
kanō da possible 50
kanojo she 2
kanojo-tachi they (referring to a group of women) 2
kanpai cheers C33
kantan da simple 50
kara from 19
kare he 2
kare-ra they 2
kariru borrow 30
kasa umbrella 70

kata Hon. person 11
katai hard 46
kata-michi one-way
ticket C9
katarogu catalogue 14
kau buy 14
kauntā counter C23
kawari ni instead of you,
etc. 67
kawase-ritsu exchange
rate 36
ka-yōbi Tuesday 27
kaze a cold; **kaze o hiku**
catch a cold 57
kazoku my, etc. family 39
keijō rieki ordinary
profit C35
keikaku plan 35
keiken experience 51
keiken suru experience 58
keiyaku contract 34
keizai taikoku great
economic country 63
keizai-gaku economics 61
kēki cake 20
kekkō da all right C19
kekkon suru get married 33
kenchiku-ka architect 3
kenka suru quarrel 72
kenkyū kaihatsu R&D 60
kenkyū suru research 61
kensaku suru search
(a database, etc.) 70
kesa this morning 37
kibishii strict 41
kieru go out/off (of electrical
device) 33
kiiroi yellow 40
kiji (newspaper) article 26
kikai chance 61
kikai machine 9
kiku ask 30

kiku hear, listen to 16
kin'en-seki non-smoking
seat C9
kinō yesterday 43
kin'yōbi Friday 27
kinyū suru fill in/out
(a form) C19
kippu ticket (train, etc.) 21
kirai da dislike (object
indicated by **ga**, not **o**) 53
kirei da beautiful 51
-kiro counter for
kilograms C24
kiru wear (of clothes) 55
kissa-ten café 23
kitai suru expect C36
kitanai dirty 46
kitsuen-seki smoking seat C9
kitte stamp 31
kōban police post 68
kochira Pol. this (one);
here C3
kochira e dōzo this way
please C17
kochira no Pol. (followed by
a noun) this C36
koe voice 55
kōen park 52
kōgi lecture 19
kōhī coffee 20
kōjō factory 26
kōkan exchange C1
kōkan-shu operator C11
koko here 4
kōkō-sei high school
student 23
kōkū-bin airmail 25
kokusai-teki da
international 50
kōkyō (no) public 56
komaru be in a fix, be a
nuisance 33

komu crowd 33
kōmu-in civil servant 1
konban this evening 64
konbenshon
convention C34
konfāmu o suru
confirm C26
konna this sort of C13
kono this, these (followed by
a noun) 9
kono chikaku near here C7
kono yō na (followed by a
noun) this sort of C36
konpyūtā computer 2
konsarutanto consultant 3
konzatsu suru get
crowded C15
kore this (one) 2
kore kara after this 11
koshō suru break down 33
kōshū denwa public
telephone 68
kotaeru answer 38
koto thing (abstract) 48
kōto coat 7
kotoshi this year C20
kowareru (something)
breaks 33
kozutsumi parcel 25
kudamono fruit 39
kudasaru Hon. (an equal or
superior) gives 62
kūkō airport 19
kūrā air-conditioner 65
kurai dark 42
kuraun (dental) crown C38
kurejitto kādo credit card 8
kureru (an equal or superior)
gives 29
kuroi black 40
kurowassan croissant C6
kuru (irreg.) come 13

kuruma car 37
kusuri medicine C38
kutsu shoes 55
kuwashii detailed;
kuwashiku in detail 57
kyanseru suru cancel 64
kyō today C5
kyōju professor 4
kyoka permission 68
kyōkai association C34
kyonen last year 30
kyū nine 8

machi street; town, city 51
machigai mistake 73
mada still, yet 33
made until, as far as 19
made ni by (a deadline) 38
mado window 54
mado-guchi (ticket)
window C2
mae: no mae ni before 55
-mae: -fun-mae (minutes)
to 18
-mae ni ago C38; before 55
magaru (something)
turns 68
mairu CV Hum. go; come 30
majime da serious (of
person) 52
man ten thousand 9
maniau be in time ('for' is
ni) 66
manyuaru manual 36
massugu ni straight
ahead C32
matsu wait 11
mazu first 36
mazui unpleasant
(to eat) 46
medama-yaki fried egg C6
meishi business card 3

nenkan uri-age-daka sales for the year C35
nenpō annual report 32
neru go to bed, sleep 27
ni at, in 23
ni to 13
ni two 8
ni de mo to ... or somewhere 65
ni tsuite about 48
nichi-yōbi Sunday 27
nigate da be weak at 53
nigiyaka da lively 51
Nihon Japan 7
Nihon'en Japanese Yen 25
Nihon-go Japanese (language) 25
Nihon-jin Japanese (person) 1
Nihon-shu sake 58
ni-mono Japanese-style boiled food C6
nimotsu luggage 23
-nin counter for people C25
ninki no takai popular C36
niwa garden 51
no of, from, 's; one 7
node so C12
nori-ba bus stop; platform C28
noru get on 31
nyūjō-ryō entrance fee C34
nyūsu news 16

o- *see following noun, verb stem or adjective*
ocha Japanese tea 15
ohiru lunch 14
ōi many 53
oishii tasty, delicious 44
okaeshi Pol. change (money) C20

o-kake ni naru Hon. sit down C17
o-kane money 21
o-kashi Japanese sweets/cakes 53
okashii funny 43
ōkii big 41
ōkime da be on the big side C36
okiru get up 27
okonau carry out, hold 26
o-konomi-yaki traditional Japanese dish slightly resembling pizza 15
okoru get angry 64
oku hundred million 9
ōku no (followed by a noun) many C36
okureru be late; **jikan ni okureru** be late 68
okuru send 13
okusan (your, etc.) wife 16
o-kyaku-sama guest; customer 29
omiyage souvenir 31
omoshiroi interesting 39
omotta hodo as I, etc. had thought 52
omou think 60
onaji same C5
onaka stomach 53
ongaku music 70
o-niku meat 37
onna no hito woman 59
orenji jūsu orange juice 20
ori-tatami-shiki (no) foldable C36
oru Hum. be 30
o-saki ni before you, etc. 37
oshieru teach; tell 65
osoi late 42

sō yū such 72
sochira Pol. that (one already mentioned); there 30
sōdan suru discuss 35
soko there (already mentioned) 4
sōmu-ka general affairs section 30
sonna ni + Neg. not so, not such a 44
sono that, those (already mentioned) (followed by a noun) 9
sono ato after that C31
sono toki then C31
sore that (one) (already mentioned) 2
sore de because of that 64
sore de wa in that case 17
sore ni sotte according to/following that C35
sōsa suru operate (a machine) 70
sotchoku da frank 63
sotsugyō suru graduate 35
subete everything 65
sugu ni immediately C17
suiei swimming 53
sui-yōbi Wednesday 27
sūji figure 52
sʉkejūru schedule C34
sʉki da like (object indicated by **ga**, not **o**) 53
sʉki-yaki Japanese grilled beef dish C33
sʉkoshi a little 21
sʉkunai few 61
sʉkʉranburudo eggu scrambled egg C6
sumimasen I'm sorry 24
sʉperu spelling C25

sʉpīchi speech; **sʉpīchi o suru** make a speech 16
sʉpōtsu sport 12
suppai sour 46
suru (irreg.) do, make 10; **ni suru** make it, decide on, have 47
sushi sushi 15
sʉteki da lovely 51
sūtsu suit 3
suu suck; **tabako o suu** smoke (cigarettes) 12
suzushii cool 43

tabako cigarette 12
taberu eat 14
tadashii correct 43
taihen very C36
taihen da awful 50
taisetsu da important 52
taishi-kan embassy 31
takʉshī taxi 25
tame ni: no tame ni for 39
tame no: no tame no for C7
tanoshii enjoyable 40
tasha Formal another company 48
tatsu stand 61
tazuneru visit 30
tēburu table C36
techō diary, personal notebook 62
tegami letter 12
tekitō da suitable 52
ten point C35
tenji-kai exhibition; trade fair 48
tenki weather 39
tenkin suru be sent to work (in another branch of a company) 73
terebi television 12

wāpuro word processor 5
warau laugh 31
warui bad 41
washoku Japanese
food C29
wasureru forget 51
watakushi Hum. I, me 30
wataru cross 68
watashi I, me 2
watashi-tachi we, us 2
wētoresu waitress C4
wisukī whisky, 70

yaki-niku grilled beef C5
yaki-tori Japanese-style
grilled chicken 53
yakusoku agreement,
promise 4; appointment 21
yakusoku o suru make an
appointment 31
yameru give up 46
yameru stop (something) 17
yaru do; play 12
yaru give (to somebody of
lower status, a plant or
animal) 62
yasashii easy; nice (of
people) 40
yasui cheap 42
yasumu rest 17
yo adds an assertive tone to
a sentence C14
yō koso welcome C27
-yō no for the use of C32
yobu call 31

yōfuku clothes 63
yoku well (irreg. adverbial
form of **ii**, 'good') 34
yomu read 12
yon four 8
yopparau get drunk;
yopparatte iru be drunk 73
yori saki ni before
(somebody) 56
yoroshii Pol. all right C9
yotei schedule C12
yōtsū lumbago C37
yoyaku reservation 31
yūbin-kyoku post office 38
yuki snow; **yuki ga furu** to
snow 49
yukkuri slowly 34
yūmei da famous 50
yushutsu kachō export
director 54
yushutsu-ka export
section 11
yuu say 29

zannen da it's a pity 66
zaseki seat C26
zasshi magazine 12
zeikin tax 9
zenbu de in all 9
zenzen + Neg. not at all 44
zero zero 8
zonjiru Hum. think 30
zutsū headache; **zutsū ga
suru** have a headache C37
zutto all the time C38

INDEX

The figures refer to Checknotes, not pages.